Bag Boutique

MAKING FABULOUS PURSES AND TOTES

Amy Barickman
and the **Indygo Junction** Design Team

Martingale ®
& COMPANY

CREDITS

President ■ Nancy J. Martin

CEO ■ Daniel J. Martin

VP and General Manager ■ Tom Wierzbicki

Publisher ■ Jane Hamada

Editorial Director ■ Mary V. Green

Managing Editor ■ Tina Cook

Technical Editor ■ Candie Frankel

Copy Editor ■ Sheila Chapman Ryan

Design Director ■ Stan Green

Illustrators ■ Jennifer Shontz and Laurel Strand

Cover and Text Designer ■ Shelly Garrison

Photographer ■ Thompson Photography

Bag Boutique: Making Fabulous Purses and Totes
© 2005 by Amy Barickman

That Patchwork Place® is an imprint of
Martingale & Company®.

Martingale & Company
20205 144th Avenue NE
Woodinville, WA 98072-8478 USA
www.martingale-pub.com

A special thanks to the designers who contributed
to this book:

■ Kathy Fernholz and Audrey Chestnut

■ Kimie Leavitt of Kimie's Quilts

■ Mary Ann Donze, designer of Indygo
Junction's Anna Claire series

Printed in China

10 09 08 07 06 05   8 7 6 5 4 3

Library of Congress Cataloging-in-Publication
Data

Barickman, Amy.
    Bag boutique : making fabulous purses and
    totes / Amy Barickman.
        p. cm.
    ISBN 1-56477-611-5
    1. Handbags. 2. Tote bags. 3. Sewing. I. Title.
    TT667.B37 2005
    646.4'8—dc22

                                2004027890

Mission Statement

Dedicated to providing quality products
and service to inspire creativity.

CONTENTS

INTRODUCTION

As any woman knows, accessories can make or break an outfit. Handbags have become the hottest accessory on the market today. Take a look around. Gone are the boring, predictable bags of the past. Stepping in and taking their place are fun, functional, one-of-a-kind bags that make a statement about who we are!

Whether you are looking for a useful everyday bag or a special occasion accessory, *Bag Boutique* has you covered. From selecting your fabric to finishing your bag, our simple step-by-step instructions will help you make a bag you can carry with pride. Choose from 15 different bag shapes and styles, then mix and match the various handle and closure options to make your own custom design. The stylish bag handles available at craft stores and online can be easily adapted to almost any of our bag patterns. We also include tips and techniques for using zippers, grommets, D rings, metal frame closures, purse feet, and magnetic snaps. Learn how to use image transfers and print to inkjet fabrics, choose an interlining, sew an interior pocket, and work with vintage fabrics and trims. It's all here!

So pour yourself a cup of coffee, sit back, and prepare to be inspired. A basic knowledge of sewing is all you need to get started. Add a little creativity and you're on your way!

—Amy Barickman and the Indygo Junction Design Team

THE BAG EXTERIOR

What kind of bag do *you* want to make? Will it be an everyday bag, or one you'll save for special occasions? Are you going for a traditional look, or something funky? The fabric used for the outside of a bag plays a starring role, so audition carefully. Here is where you cast the bag's ultimate look and style.

For an everyday bag, consider hardwearing fabrics such as quilting cottons, upholstery, home decorating fabrics, and canvas. For a special occasion bag, spring for something luxurious. Sensuous textures such as silk, suede, brocade, and velvet will add to your ensemble and your enjoyment. A purse requires such a small amount of fabric that you won't have to spend a fortune to get that million-dollar look.

To inspire your most creative sewing, don't limit yourself to fabrics purchased off the bolt. Do you have a favorite dress, skirt, or sweater that you can no longer wear but aren't ready to give up? Cut it up and use it to make a purse. Shop thrift stores for nifty fabrics you can recycle. Remember to check the remnant bins at the fabric store. Fabrics you might not ordinarily choose—such as vinyl, oilcloth, border prints, wool, and chenille—will give your bag a fun look. A little piece is all you need.

TIP: Don't be afraid to use a large-scale print on a small bag. The results can be outrageous!

Embellishments

Trims and embellishments will take your bag over the top! Ostrich feathers, fur, rhinestones, ribbons, rickrack—you're sure to find treasures in the marketplace to rev up your design. Ribbon-type trims can run around the top edge of a bag, pop out of seams, and decorate tabs. If you don't like the color of a trim's supporting tape, cover it up with a pretty ribbon or hide it in a seam. Bugle beads, sequins, and seed beads can be attached with craft glue or fusible products such as Steam-A-Seam. Use your imagination and don't be afraid to try something new!

IMAGE TRANSFERS

Printed images are an easy way to add punch and personality to a plain bag. Images can be printed directly to fabric or they can be made into iron-on transfers. For both methods, you'll use an inkjet printer and your home computer. Iron-on transfers are handy when you want to put an image on a bag but don't want to embellish it with stitching. It's a clean, no-fuss look. If decorative stitching will add some extra punch to your bag, then print the image to a fabric sheet and attach it to the bag with decorative machine stitches. Images printed to fabric sheets are more textured than those printed with iron-on transfers.

The images used in this book are from The Vintage Workshop®. You can download them free of charge at www.thevintageworkshop.com. The images are also included in *Chic Bag Boutique*, *Clothing Collage*, and *The Little Ones*, three Click-n-Craft CD-ROM collections from The Vintage Workshop.

Printing an Image

To print on fabric, you will need:

- The image specified in the project directions, available on CD or online. For free image download, go to www.thevintageworkshop.com, click on Special Promotions, and enter PRS123 as your source code.

- Computer and inkjet printer

- Click-n-Craft® Cotton Poplin or Cotton Canvas fabric sheet

- Steam-A-Seam fusible web

- Iron

- Scissors

1. Print the image onto a fabric sheet, following the instructions on the fabric packaging.

2. Use scissors to cut out the printed image directly on the outline or ¼" beyond the outline, following the project instructions.

3. Remove the paper backing from the fabric sheet. If you added a ¼" margin in step 2, turn it to the wrong side and press.

4. Apply Steam-A-Seam fusible web to the back of the fabric image, following the manufacturer's instructions.

5. Remove the paper backing from the fusible web. Place the image on the project fabric, right side up. Fuse in place. Add decorative machine stitching if desired.

Making an Iron-On Transfer

To print an iron-on transfer, you will need:

- The image specified in the project directions, available on CD or online. For free image download, go to www.thevintageworkshop.com, click on Special Promotions, and enter PRS123 as your source code.

- Computer and inkjet printer

- Click-n-Craft Iron-On Transfer II (includes parchment pressing sheet)

- Iron

- Scissors

1. Print the image onto an iron-on transfer sheet, following the manufacturer's directions on the packaging.

2. Use scissors to cut out the image on the outline.

3. Remove the paper backing. Place the iron-on transfer face down on the project fabric. Lay the parchment pressing sheet on top. Press with a dry iron, following the manufacturer's directions, to complete the transfer.

CLOSURES

Closures, frames, and handles help determine the form and functionality of a bag.

Bag closures run the gamut, from simple fold-over flaps to magnetic catches. In this section we outline the many ways you can keep a bag closed.

Flaps and Tabs

A flap or tab is an easy way to add pizzazz to a plain bag. A flap runs the full length of the bag opening and helps keep the bag contents secure. A tab is narrower and gives a more casual, open look to the top of the bag.

You can design the size and shape of a flap or tab any way you like. Fold in the corners of a rectangular flap and tack them down to make a triangular flap. To secure a flap, you can add a decorative buckle, a button, or a hidden

closure on the underside. Another option is to put a snap on the top inside edge of the bag and allow the flap to fall over the front. On a plain flap, try an antique brooch or pin. It will make an attractive embellishment, and the added weight will help a loose flap stay closed.

Classy Hardware

Snap-ring closures, D rings, grommets, and buckles are visible, jazzy closures for your bags. A snap ring is a hook that can be clicked open to attach to a D ring or grommet. A D ring is shaped like the letter D and can be made of metal or plastic. A grommet is used to reinforce a hole made in the fabric. By using snap rings in conjunction with

D rings or grommets you can achieve a secure closure. Another way to close a bag is to thread a cord or rope through a series of grommets and pull the bag closed.

Buttons

Buttons are like jewelry on a purse. Large one-of-a-kind vintage buttons, fabric-covered buttons, and other treasures from your button box add pizzazz as well as function. Garage sales and estate sales often have fun pieces of jewelry that can be used as buttons.

A simple button-down flap helps keep the purse's contents secure. If a button is too bulky or ornate to pass through a buttonhole (or if you simply don't like sewing buttonholes), sew the button directly to the flap and add a hidden closure underneath. No one will ever know the difference. A bag with an open top can be made more secure with a loop-and-button closure. Make the loop from cording, ribbon, or a narrow tube of fabric. Baste the loop to the right side of the bag back before joining the lining. Sew the button to the bag front.

Hidden Closures

Hidden closures, such as snaps and Velcro hook-and-loop tabs, are convenient to use and give a bag a professionally made look. A magnetic snap secured in the lining lets you open and close a bag quickly— a very practical piece of hardware to have on a bag that you'll open dozens of times a day. Bags made with metal hex-open and tubular frames snap open for easy removal of contents and just as easily snap shut. You have the security of closing a bag and knowing it will stay closed.

Inserting Magnetic Snaps:

To insert a magnetic snap, you will need:

- Magnetic snap—two halves plus disks (for lightweight lining fabric), or two halves plus two 1" x 1" squares of lightweight plastic needle-point canvas or milk-jug plastic (for heavyweight lining fabrics)

- Two pieces, 1½" x 1½", of fusible interfacing

- Craft knife or small, sharp scissors

- Iron

- Pencil

- Ruler

1. Use a ruler and pencil to measure and mark the center top edge of each bag lining. Measure down 1" (1½" if the finished edge will be topstitched) from this mark and make a second mark. Repeat on the reverse side of each lining.

2. Lay the linings wrong side up. Center a fusible interfacing square on the second mark on each lining. Fuse in place.

3. Layer the linings wrong sides together. Center a snap on the second mark (on the right side of the fabric). Make two little marks where the snap prongs touch the fabric. Using a craft knife or small, sharp scissors, cut a tiny slit at each mark through both layers. Separate the linings.

4. *For lightweight linings:* Insert the snap prongs through the slits from the right side. Turn the lining over. Slip a disk onto the back of the snap. To secure the disk, bend the prongs toward the center of the disk, pressing against a hard, flat surface.

    For heavyweight linings: Center a snap on each 1" x 1" plastic square. Mark the plastic where the prongs will enter. Cut a tiny slit at each mark. Insert the snap prongs through the slits in the lining fabric from the right side. Turn the lining over. Slip a plastic square onto the prongs. Bend the prongs toward the outside edge of the square, pressing against a hard, flat surface.

5. After the bag is assembled, tack the lining to the main bag fabric on each side of the snap. The plastic pieces help prevent wear and tear on heavyweight fabrics such as denim.

Inserting a Metal Hex-Open Frame:

To install a hex-open frame, you will need:

- Metal hex-open frame (see "Resources" on page 96)

- Small pliers

- Handbag with casing for frame

Follow the manufacturer's instructions to put the frame together and add the pins *without* the purse fabric. Doing a dry run will help you understand how the frame operates. When you do the final assembly, you want to make sure the purse snaps closed in the right direction.

If you have difficulty lining up the loops where the pin goes, the middle prong may need adjusting. Use small pliers to gently bend up the middle prong just a little. The idea is to allow more room for the loops to line up so that the pin slides in evenly. Play with the frame to see how this works.

When you're ready, slide the frame into the bag casing one side at a time. Make sure that the ends line up properly, and then slide in the pin. Be patient! Inserting a hex-open frame requires manual dexterity but the results are worth it.

Inserting a Tubular Frame:

To install a tubular frame, you will need:

- Metal tubular frame (see "Resources" on page 96)
- Small pliers
- Handbag with casing for frame

Follow the manufacturer's instructions to put the frame together *without* the purse fabric. After you've accomplished a successful dry run and you understand how the frame works, add the purse and complete the assembly.

❦ HANDLES AND STRAPS ❦

The handle styles on our bags fall into two categories: purchased handles and fabric straps, including shoulder straps. Each type has its own look and characteristics.

Purchased Handles

Almost any craft or fabric store has purse handles available for purchase. Most handles are made of hard plastic or plastic made to look like wood or bamboo. Tabs or casings connect the handles to the bags; if you are uncertain which connector to choose, find a bag with a similar handle in the book and follow those instructions for making your tabs or casing. As long as you are careful about centering the handle on your chosen bag, you have a lot of choices for your bag shape.

Fabric Handles and Straps

Many of our bag patterns can be made with fabric handles or shoulder straps instead of purchased handles. To make a flat, padded shoulder strap, like the kind you see on many purchased fabric handbags, you will need extra purse fabric (or contrasting fabric) and fusible batting. After you sew the straps, pin them to the bag and adjust the length to your liking. You can easily customize the instructions to make shorter or longer handles or a wide single strap that attaches to the bag at the side seams. Another design option, featured on the Pocketbook Purse (page 62), is to use bias-cut fabric strips for the purse trim and handle. On curved edges, bias strips

provide the necessary give and stretch that a straight-cut binding strip cannot. Plaids and striped fabrics cut on the bias take on a new design dimension.

Making Shoulder Straps:

To make shoulder straps, you will need:

- 2 strips of fabric, 3" x 29"
- 4 strips of fusible batting, 1¼" x 29"
- Iron
- Press cloth
- Safety pin
- Sewing machine

1. Fold a fabric strip in half lengthwise, right sides together. Stitch the long edges together using a ¼" seam allowance.

2. Turn the casing right side out. Press, centering the seam.

3. Layer two batting strips, fusible sides together. Lay a press cloth on top and press to fuse.

4. Attach a safety pin to the batting strip and draw it through the casing by pulling on the pin. Remove the safety pin, and adjust and straighten the batting as needed.

5. Stitch down the middle of the strap and ¼" from each long edge. Repeat to make two straps.

Making a Bias Strip:

To make a bias fabric strip, suitable for purse trim or handles, you will need:

■ Square or rectangle of fabric, at least 18" x 22"

■ Rotary cutter, ruler, and cutting mat

■ Sewing machine

1. Starting at the bottom left corner of the fabric, measure an equal distance along the bottom and left edges and make a mark on each edge. The distance you measure will depend on the size of the fabric. Align the ruler on the marks. Run the rotary cutter along the edge of the ruler, making a diagonal cut across the fabric.

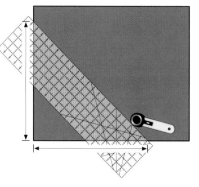

2. Align the ruler on the cut edge to cut a strip to the width specified in the project instructions. For example, in the Pocketbook Purse, page 62, the bias strips are cut 3½" wide.

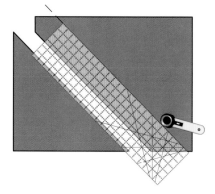

3. Trim both ends of the strip on the lengthwise grain of the fabric.

4. Repeat steps 2 and 3 to cut multiple strips as needed. Sew the strips together end to end, using a ¼" seam allowance. Press the seam allowance open.

INSIDE THE BAG

The inside of your handbag is your private domain. The right lining fabric can cheer you up. The right pockets keep you organized. The right interlining provides body and structure and makes you feel good, too. Strive for the same quality materials and workmanship inside the bag as you do outside the bag, and you won't be disappointed.

Lining

The fabric on the inside of the bag plays a supporting role. Loud or busy patterns can add just the right touch of whimsy to an otherwise conservative bag. It's fun to open a prim and proper bag and find a splash of color inside. Some linings spill over onto the outside of the bag in the form of contrast bands. When you find a successful bag and lining combination to make a reversible bag, you truly will have two bags for the price of one.

Cotton fabrics make practical, attractive linings, especially in larger bags, because of their light weight and extensive color and pattern choices. Heavier tapestry and upholstery fabrics can be used

too. In a smaller bag, the trick is to avoid a lot of bulky lining seams. Nylon linings are thinner than cotton and help reduce bulk. They are particularly useful on bags that are interlined.

Interlining

The interlining is a material that is sandwiched between the main fabric and the lining to give the bag shape and stability. Various materials can be used. You must take into consideration the weight of the lining and bag fabrics, as well as the size and function of the bag, in order to choose an appropriate interlining. The sandwiched layers should be sturdy but not too bulky.

An interlining can be basted or fused in place. Basting is generally sufficient for small bags, but in large bags, fusing provides added stability. You can use self-fusibles, such as fusible batting or fusible interfacing, or you can choose another material for the interlining and apply fusible web to one side. To reduce bulk in the seam allowance, trim a fusible interlining to ⅛" outside the sewing line. If the bag seam allowance is ½", for example,

you would trim off ⅜" from the interlining seam allowance. Place the interlining on the wrong side of the bag fabric, aligning the sewing lines, and fuse in place.

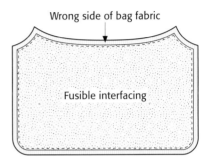

Wrong side of bag fabric

Fusible interfacing

Batting: Use quilt batting as an interlining when you want to quilt the fabric layers together. Batting can also help support decorative stitching. For small or lightweight bags, use one layer of regular quilt batting. On larger bags, try fusible fleece to prevent the layers from shifting. Fuse the fleece to the wrong side of the bag fabric before stitching. You can even fuse two batting layers together for extra durability and weight.

TIP: Use a press cloth or a Teflon iron plate (which slips over your regular iron) when applying fusible fleece. Don't allow the fusing agent to get on your iron.

Nonwoven Interfacing:
Interfacing is a nonwoven fabric that is available in many weights. It lets you add weight and support without the bulk of batting. As a general rule, choose a lightweight interfacing for a small bag and a heavier interfacing for a larger bag. If both the bag fabric and the lining fabric are heavy, a lightweight interfacing may be sufficient to give body to the the bag. Fusible interfacings are especially easy to use.

Timtex Interfacing: Timtex interfacing is used commercially in handbags and is an excellent product for stiffening the sides and bottoms of the handbags you make yourself. It allows the bag to truly stand up on its own. Do not use Timtex to interline facings, handles, or other small pieces, however. It will make them uncomfortably stiff. After your bag is completed, give it a good pressing and it will hold the shape.

Canvas: Lightweight cotton canvas can make a suitable interlining on a large bag. It adds body without stiffness. It can be basted or fused to the bag fabric.

Inside Pockets

What is a handbag without an inside pocket? Your cell phone, keys, and that extra tube of lipstick deserve a place of their own to help you stay organized. The pocket size and shape depend on the size of the bag and your personal preference and needs. If a pocket is too wide, it can flop open and spill its contents. A few stitches down the center will secure the pocket to the lining and create separate compartments. Don't place a pocket too close to the top of a bag or it may interfere with the closure. The pocket fabric can match the lining or contrast with it.

To make an inside pocket, you will need:

- Fabric for pocket
- Paper
- Pencil
- Pins
- Ruler
- Scissors

1. Decide the dimensions of the finished pocket. Use a ruler and pencil to draw a square or rectangle this size on paper. Add 1" to the top edge and ¼" to the side and bottom edges. Cut out the paper pattern.

2. Pin the pattern to the pocket fabric (generally, you would use the lining fabric). Cut out the shape with scissors. Sew a zigzag stitch around the side and bottom edges.

3. Fold and press the side and bottom edges of the pocket ¼" to the wrong side. Press the top edge ½" to the wrong side twice to make a double-fold hem. Topstitch the first fold of the double-fold hem through all layers.

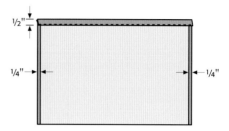

4. Center the pocket on the lining, right sides up. Topstitch the side and bottom edges. Stitch again ¼" from the edge.

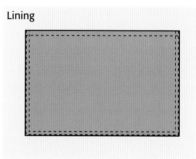

5. Stitch one or more vertical stitching lines to divide the pocket into compartments.

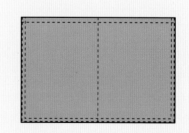

Bottom Inserts

To prevent flat-bottomed bags from sagging, we like to install a piece of heavyweight plastic needlepoint canvas, cut to fit the bag bottom. It is always better to cut the plastic canvas slightly larger than the bag bottom, and trim it to fit.

To make a bottom insert, you will need:

- Heavyweight plastic needle-point canvas
- Paper or paper pattern
- Pencil (optional)
- Ruler
- Scissors
- Needle
- Thread

1. *If there is a pattern for the fabric bag bottom:* Make a copy of the pattern. Cut slightly beyond the stitching line to make a pattern for the insert.

   If there is no pattern for the bag bottom: Turn the bag upside down and use a measuring tape to measure the bottom of the bag. Use a ruler and pencil to draw a shape about ¼" larger than the bag bottom on all sides. Cut on the marked line to make a pattern for the insert.

2. Use the pattern prepared in step 1 to cut a shape from plastic needlepoint canvas.

3. Test-fit the plastic canvas in the bottom of the bag. Trim as needed. The fit should be snug, but it should not stretch or distort the bag fabric.

4. Turn the bag inside out. Using a needle and thread, tack the canvas to the bag bottom every 2" or so.

YARDAGE AND ASSEMBLY

General Supplies

You'll need the supplies listed below for all of the projects in this book.

- Needles
- Pins
- Rotary cutter, ruler, and mat
- Scissors
- Sewing machine
- Steam iron
- Thread

A few projects call for a serger; if you don't have one, overcast the raw edges with a zigzag stitch instead. A pressing sleeve is useful when a purse opening is too small to fit over the tapered end of a standard ironing board.

Yardage Requirements

The bag and lining fabric requirements are based on a 42" width of yardage. If you are recycling fabric from a piece of clothing or a remnant that is not 42" wide, you will need to take the actual fabric width into account.

The interlining yardage requirement is the same as for the bag fabric. Unfortunately, the interlinings we recommend (see "Interlining" on page 11) come in various widths, and we could not realistically provide yardage requirements for all of them.

Timtex is 22" wide, fusible interfacing is typically 22" wide, fusible batting is 45" wide, and canvas is 42" to 60" wide.

The best way to gauge how much of a particular interlining you need is to lay out the interlining and place the bag patterns on it. You would probably be doing this anyway if, like us, you are pulling potential candidates from your stash. Remember to allow for pattern pieces that are cut on a fold or cut in duplicate when making your estimate. A medium-sized bag cut from ¾ yard of 42"-wide fabric can easily require two yards of 22"-wide Timtex to interline it. Use the same method to gauge the amount of Steam-A-Seam fusible web needed to fuse an interlining to the bag fabric.

Cutting and Marking

Patterns for the bags are printed in the book either actual size or to be enlarged on a photocopier. Most of the bag projects use at least one printed pattern. Simple shapes, like squares and rectangles, are cut with a rotary cutter and ruler. The cutting instructions explain how many pieces to cut, piece sizes, and which fabrics to use. For fast, accurate cutting, stack fabrics and cut through multiple layers. Label the pieces as you cut them so you don't get confused.

To use a printed pattern, make a photocopy of it, enlarging if directed. Follow the notes on the pattern to layer or fold the fabric. Pin or weight the pattern to the fabric and then cut on the pattern outline through all the layers using scissors or a rotary cutter. Another method is to transfer the pattern to the reverse side of the fabric using a tracing wheel and dressmaker's tracing paper. Choose a method that is comfortable for you and works well with your fabric.

Some of the patterns have markings, such as dots or placement lines, that are essential to accurate construction of the bag. Transfer all the markings to the bag fabric before you begin sewing. As a general rule, mark the fabric pieces immediately after you cut them, while the pattern is still pinned to the fabric. If the interlining will be fused to the bag pieces, complete the fusing first and then do the marking.

Marking with Dressmaker's Tracing Paper:

Use dressmaker's tracing paper to mark fold lines, tucks, buttonholes, and the placement lines for pockets, tabs, and flaps. A package of tracing paper includes several colors; choose a color that contrasts with the fabric being marked. Test the product on scrap fabric, following the manufacturer's instructions, to make sure the markings really will rub or wash out. If in doubt, mark only on the wrong side of the fabric.

To mark the fabric, you will need:

- Dressmaker's tracing paper
- Serrated tracing wheel
- Clear ruler (from your rotary-cutting set)
- Scissors

1. Cut a piece of tracing paper slightly larger than the pattern marking.

2. Insert the paper, coated side down, between the pattern and the fabric so that it is directly under the pattern marking. The fabric can be a double layer. You can remove a few pins from the pattern if necessary.

3. Align the ruler on the pattern marking.

4. Roll the tracing wheel along the edge of the ruler, as you would a rotary cutter, starting and stopping exactly on the pattern marking.

5. Unpin and remove the pattern. Separate the two fabric pieces. The serrated tracing wheel allows the powdery coating to penetrate down through the double fabric layer so each piece is marked.

Marking with Tailor's Chalk:

Use tailor's chalk on the right or wrong side of the fabric. It brushes right off. Some chalks come with holders, making them easier to use. Each piece of fabric must be marked separately with the chalk.

To mark fabric, you will need:

- Tailor's chalk
- Clear ruler (from your rotary-cutting set)

1. Fold the pattern back on itself, right sides together, along the marking line. You can remove a few pins from the pattern if necessary.

2. Align the ruler on the pattern marking.

3. Run the edge of the tailor's chalk along the edge of the ruler, starting and stopping exactly on the pattern marking. Unpin and remove the pattern or, if there are more lines on the pattern to be marked, restore the pattern to its initial position and reinsert the pins.

4. Repeat steps 1–3 for each line to be marked.

Joining the Lining

There are several ways to line a bag. The particular method you choose depends on the design of the bag. One way is to insert the lining in the bag when the bag is finished. The top raw edges can then be bound or folded in, pressed, and topstitched from the right side.

An easier way, described below, is to leave an opening in one of the lining seams and to sew the top raw edges of the lining and the bag together. Any tabs or handles that were basted to the top outside edge of the bag get sewn into the seam.

Follow these steps to join the lining to the bag.

1. Turn the bag inside out. Tuck the handles and tabs down into the bag, out of the way.

2. Turn the lining right side out. (Make sure you have left an opening in the lining bottom for turning.)

3. Insert the lining into the bag, right sides together and seams aligned. Pin around the top edge.

4. Stitch all around using the seam allowance specified for the project. Only the basted ends of the handles and straps should be caught in the seams.

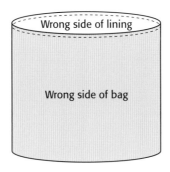

5. Pull the bag through the opening in the lining and turn both sections right side out. Slip-stitch the opening.

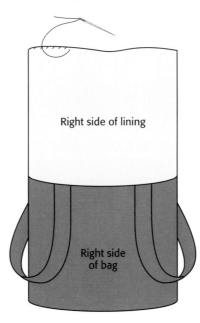

6. Tuck the lining down inside the bag. Press the top edge.

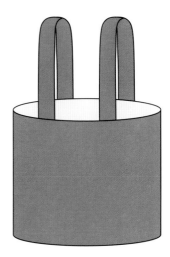

Final Tacking

Tacking is a strictly utilitarian stitch, done by hand with a needle and thread. The idea is to take small, discreet stitches to secure the lining to the bag at points of stress. These strategic areas include the bottom corners and edges, the corners of inside pockets, and around the magnetic snap. Any stitches that hold the lining in place can be used. Tacking doesn't have to be beautiful, just functional and unobtrusive. If the bag is reversible, choose a thread color that will be invisible from both sides.

❧ FLARE BAG ❧

FLARE BAG

MATERIALS

The yardage is based on a 42" width. In addition to the items below, you'll need the general supplies listed on page 13.

- ⅝ yard of fabric for bag and handle tabs
- ½ yard of fabric for lining and pockets
- ½ yard of interlining
- Scraps of red wool for flower and closure tabs
- Scrap of green wool for leaf
- Black pom-pom
- 5" x 5" piece of lightweight fusible interfacing
- Velcro hook-and-loop tape, ½" x 1½", separated
- Purchased handles
- Heavyweight plastic needlepoint canvas

CUTTING

See "Cutting and Marking" on page 14. Transfer the pattern markings to the fabric pieces before you begin sewing.

From the bag fabric, cut:
2 pieces using the front and back pattern (page 22)
4 squares, 2⅜" x 2⅜", for handle tabs

The roomy flare silhouette is a handbag classic. Press the folds to emphasize the angled sides or leave them loose for a casual tote. Complete the look with purchased clutch handles and decorative trims, such as the dimensional poppy shown here. The bag measures 11" x 8", with a 3"-deep base.

16

From the interlining, cut:

2 pieces using the front and back pattern

From the lining fabric, cut:

2 pieces using the front and back pattern

From the fusible interfacing, cut:

4 squares, 2⅜" x 2⅜", for handle tabs

From the red wool, cut:

2 pieces, 1⅝" x 3¼", for closure tabs

3 pieces using the flower patterns (page 21), 1 of each size

From the green wool, cut:

1 piece using the leaf pattern (page 21), fringing the edges as marked on the pattern

ASSEMBLY

1. Fuse or baste an interlining piece to the wrong side of a bag-fabric piece. Make two.

2. Layer the interlined bag pieces right sides together. Stitch the side and bottom edges using a ½" seam allowance. Do not stitch the cutout corners. Press the seams open.

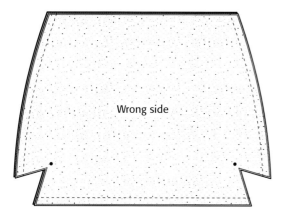

Wrong side

3. To form the bottom corners, refold the bag, right sides together, aligning a side seam on the bottom seam. Stitch the raw edges from dot to dot, using a ¼" seam allowance.

Repeat to box the other corner. Turn right side out. Press.

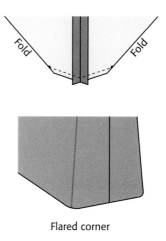

Flared corner

4. Add a pocket to one or both of the lining pieces, if desired. (See "Inside Pockets" on page 12.) Join the lining pieces as in step 2, leaving 4" open in the bottom seam for turning. Sew the lining corners as in step 3.

5. Fuse a handle tab interfacing piece to the wrong side of a matching fabric piece. Fold the piece in half, right sides together. Stitch the edges opposite the fold using a ¼" seam allowance. Turn right side out. Press, centering the seam. Make four handle tabs.

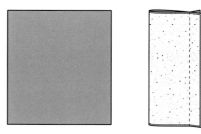

Make 4.

6. Slip a tab through, or fold it over, one end of a handle. Bring the raw edges of the tab together, keeping the seam on the inside, and baste closed. Repeat for each tab. Pin the tabs to the top outside edge of the bag,

raw edges aligned, so that the handles are centered on the bag front and bag back. Baste.

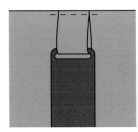

7. Fold a closure tab piece in half lengthwise, right sides together. Stitch the long edge and one short edge using a ¼" seam allowance. Trim the excess seam allowance at the corners. Turn right side out and press. Make two closure tabs.

8. Pin the closure tabs to the top outside edge of the bag at each side seam, raw edges aligned. Baste. Stand the bag upright. Pull each closure tab toward the center until the finished ends overlap by 1½". Pin the Velcro pieces to each tab as shown. Machine stitch around the edges of each Velcro piece.

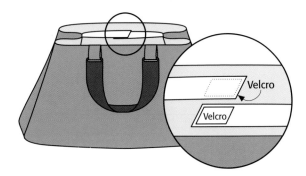

9. Add a plastic canvas insert to the bottom of the bag. (See "Bottom Inserts" on page 13.) Join and tack the lining. (See "Joining the Lining" on page 15 and "Final Tacking" on page 15.)

10. Layer the flowers from largest to smallest. Tack them to the bag just below one of the handle tabs. Fold the leaf in half. Tack it under the flower on one side.

11. Sew on a black pom-pom for the flower center.

Shoe Flare Bag

This glittery silk shantung bag pokes fun at the fashion rule that says shoes and a bag must match. Use your computer, inkjet printer, and a free image download to make the shoe appliqué. (Image is also available on the *Chic Bag Boutique* Click-n-Craft CD-ROM from The Vintage Workshop.) Decorate the shoe with small assorted silver beads, bugle beads, and sequins. You'll also need a ¾-yard feather boa with rhinestones and white craft glue. Follow "Cutting" on page 16, omitting the flower and leaf pieces.

1. Download the shoe image (go to www.thevintageworkshop.com, click on Special Promotions, and enter PRS123 as your source code) or select it from the *Chic Bag Boutique* CD. Print two shoe images, one on a Click-n-Craft Cotton Poplin sheet and one on plain paper. (See "Printing an Image" on page 6.)

2. Following the manufacturer's instructions, apply paper-backed fusible web to the back of the poplin sheet. Cut out the shoe directly on the outline to make a fusible appliqué.

3. Cut out the shoe toe from the paper photocopy and then trace the shape onto fusible web. Cut out the toe.

4. Complete "Assembly" step 1 on page 17. Fuse the shoe appliqué to the bag front. Align and fuse the fusible web toe cutout to the shoe appliqué. Remove the paper from the toe. Spread an even layer of assorted beads on the toe, place a sheet of paper on top, and steam with an iron until the beads adhere, about 20 seconds. Let cool. To avoid melting beads, do not touch the iron directly to them; use paper as a pressing cloth.

5. Brush off any loose beads. Use white craft glue to affix bugle beads in the empty spaces on the toe. Glue silver sequins to alternate dots on the polka-dot portion of the shoe.

6. Follow "Assembly" steps 2–8. If you've chosen curlicue handles like the ones in the photo, remove them after step 6 and then reinsert them after the bag has been completed. Complete step 9, creasing the fold lines to set the flare at the corners of the bag. Finish the bag with the trims.

TIP: The feather boa and beads were purchased as one trim. If you would like to use more than one kind of trim, simply layer them. Glue the trims in place with a good-quality fabric glue.

Umbrella Lady Flare Bag

Soft, muted tones characterize this vintage image, which you can download and print onto fabric. (Image is also available on the *Chic Bag Boutique* Click-n-Craft CD-ROM from The Vintage Workshop.) This bag variation omits the closure tabs for a less exaggerated flare and uses two handle tabs instead of four to attach the handles. Follow "Cutting" on page 16, with the following changes:

■ On the bag front and back, do not mark the flare fold lines.

■ Omit the closure tabs and flower and leaf pieces.

■ Omit the 2¾" x 2⅜" handle tabs. Instead, cut two pieces, 4" x 10½", from the bag fabric and two matching pieces from the interfacing for the handle tabs.

1. Download the umbrella lady image (go to www.thevintageworkshop.com, click on Special Promotions, and enter PRS123 as your source code). Print it onto a Click-n-Craft Cotton Poplin sheet. (See "Printing an Image" on page 6.)

2. Cut out the image, allowing a ¼" margin all around, and press the seam allowances to the back. Following the manufacturer's instructions, apply paper-backed fusible web to the back of the poplin sheet.

3. Complete "Assembly" step 1 on page 17. Fuse the image to the bag. Set your sewing machine for a decorative stitch. Stitch around the outside edge of the appliqué in contrasting thread.

4. Follow "Assembly" steps 2–4.

5. Fuse a handle tab interfacing piece to the wrong side of a matching fabric piece. Fold in half, right sides together. Stitch the edge opposite the fold using a ¼" seam allowance. Turn right side out. Press, centering the seam. Make two handle tabs.

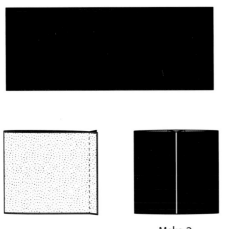

Make 2.

6. Fold a tab over one handle. Bring the raw edges together, with the seam on the inside, and baste closed. Repeat. Pin the tabs to the top outside edge of the bag, raw edges aligned, so that the handles are centered on the bag front and bag back. Baste.

7. Follow "Assembly" step 9 to complete the bag.

Tapestry Flare Bag

Create this tapestry look using a floral print bark cloth or a similar medium-weight decorator fabric. Follow "Cutting" on page 16, omitting the flower and leaf pieces.

1. Follow "Assembly" steps 1–5 on page 17. At the end of step 5, tuck in the raw edges of the handle tabs. Press.

2. Slip a tab through, or fold it over, one end of a handle. Bring the tucked ends of the tab together, with the seam on the inside, and baste closed. Repeat for each tab. Pin the tabs to the outside of the bag, centering the handles, so the base of the handles will fall about 1½" below the finished edge of the bag. Baste. Topstitch along the tucked edges. If you've chosen curlicue handles like the ones in the photo, remove them after sewing the tabs to the bag and reinsert them after the bag is completed.

3. Follow "Assembly" steps 7–9, creasing the fold lines to set the flare at the corners of the bag. For a softer look at the base, omit the bottom insert.

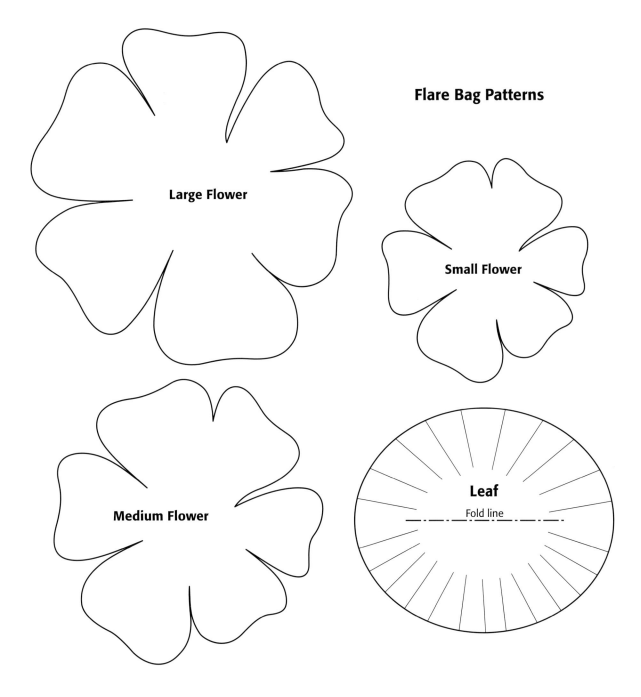

Flare Bag Patterns

Large Flower

Small Flower

Medium Flower

Leaf

Fold line

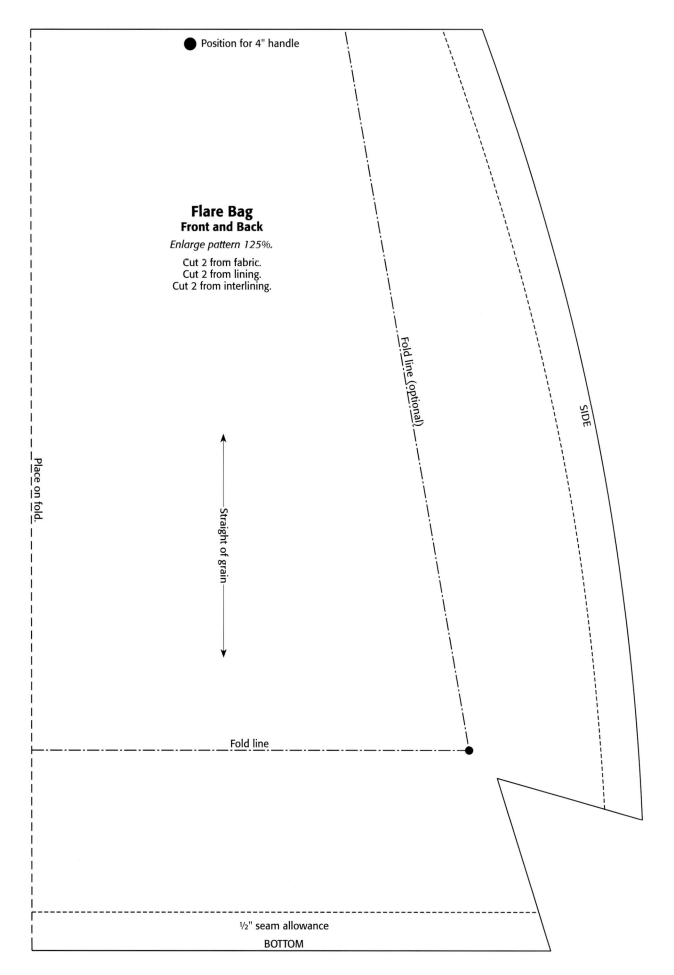

● Position for 4" handle

Flare Bag
Front and Back

Enlarge pattern 125%.

Cut 2 from fabric.
Cut 2 from lining.
Cut 2 from interlining.

Fold line (optional)

SIDE

Place on fold.

Straight of grain

Fold line

½" seam allowance

BOTTOM

Naomi Bag

HYDRANGEA NAOMI BAG

The wide, open top and straight handles of this bag make it easy to reach in for your sunglasses or car keys. The sides flare up and out for a casual silhouette. Try curved handles for a different look. The bag measures 11" x 10" x 6" deep.

MATERIALS

The yardage is based on a 42" width unless otherwise noted. In addition to the items below, you'll need the general supplies listed on page 13.

- ⅝ yard of fabric for bag
- ½ yard of fabric for lining and pockets
- ½ yard of interlining
- ⅜ yard of lightweight fusible interfacing, 22" wide
- Purchased straight handles, 11¾"
- Magnetic snap closure (optional)
- Heavyweight plastic needlepoint canvas

CUTTING

See "Cutting and Marking" on page 14. Transfer the pattern markings to the fabric pieces before you begin sewing.

From the bag fabric, cut:
2 pieces using the front and back pattern (page 26)
4 pieces, 5⅜" x 8", for handle tabs

From the interlining, cut:
2 pieces using the front and back pattern

From the lining fabric, cut:
2 pieces using the front and back pattern

From the fusible interfacing, cut:
4 pieces, 5⅜" x 8", for handle tabs

ASSEMBLY

1. Fuse or baste an interlining piece to the wrong side of a bag-fabric piece. Make two.

2. Layer the interlined bag pieces right sides together. Stitch the side and bottom edges using a ¼" seam allowance. Do not stitch the cutout corners. Press the seams open.

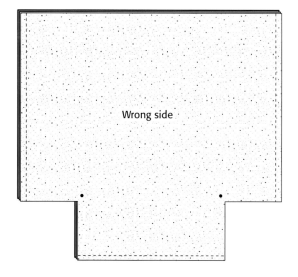

Wrong side

3. To form the bottom corners, refold the bag, right sides together, aligning a side seam on the bottom seam. Stitch the raw edges from dot to dot using a ¼" seam allowance. Repeat to box the other corner. Turn right side out. Press.

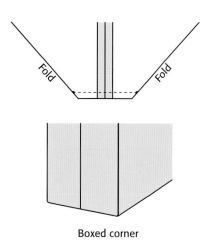

Boxed corner

4. Add a pocket to one or both of the lining pieces if desired. (See "Inside Pockets" on page 12.) Add a magnetic snap closure to the lining if desired. (See "Inserting Magnetic Snaps" on page 8.) Join the lining pieces as in step 2, leaving 6" open in the bottom seam for turning. Sew the lining corners as in step 3.

5. Fuse a handle-tab interfacing piece to the wrong side of a matching fabric piece. Fold in half, right sides together. Stitch the edge opposite the fold using a ¼" seam allowance. Turn right side out. Press, centering the seam. Make four handle tabs.

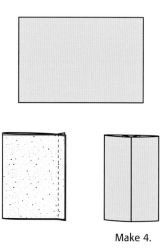

Make 4.

6. Fold each handle tab in half, with the seam on the inside, and baste the raw edges together. Pin two handle tabs to the top outside edges of the bag front between the dots, raw edges aligned. Baste. Repeat for the bag back.

7. Add a plastic canvas insert to the bottom of the bag. (See "Bottom Inserts" on page 13.) Join and tack the lining. (See "Joining the Lining" on page 15 and "Final Tacking" on page 15.)

8. Stitch across each handle tab, 1" from the folded edge, to make a casing. Insert the straight handles.

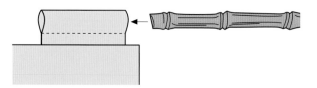

Banded Naomi Bag

Three coordinating fabrics make this bag fun inside and out. We chose an oversized floral print, a plaid, and a red check. The beaded handles are attached to two wide tabs at the middle of the bag. Follow "Cutting" on page 23 with the following changes:

- From the floral print, cut two pieces using the front and back pattern.
- From the plaid (for the lining), cut two pieces using the front and back pattern.
- From the red check, cut two pieces using the contrast band pattern.
- Omit the 5⅜" x 8" handle tabs. Instead cut two pieces, 3¼" x 9¼", from the red check for the handle tabs. Cut two matching pieces from the fusible interfacing.

1. Complete step 1 of "Assembly" on page 24. Press ¼" of the long edge of the contrast band to the wrong side. Place the contrast band on the bag front, matching the side and bottom edges. Topstitch the folded edge. Baste the raw edges. Repeat for the bag back.

Make 2.

2. Follow "Assembly" steps 2–4.

3. Fuse a handle-tab interfacing piece to the wrong side of a matching fabric piece. Fold in half, right sides together. Stitch the edge opposite the fold using a ¼" seam allowance. Turn right side out. Press, centering the seam. Make two handle tabs.

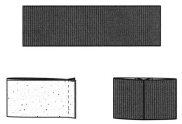

Make 2.

4. Fold a tab over one handle. Bring the raw edges of the tab together, with the seam on the inside, and baste closed. Repeat. Pin the tabs to the top outside edge of the bag, raw edges aligned, so that the handles are centered on the bag front and bag back. Baste.

5. Follow "Assembly" step 7 to complete the bag.

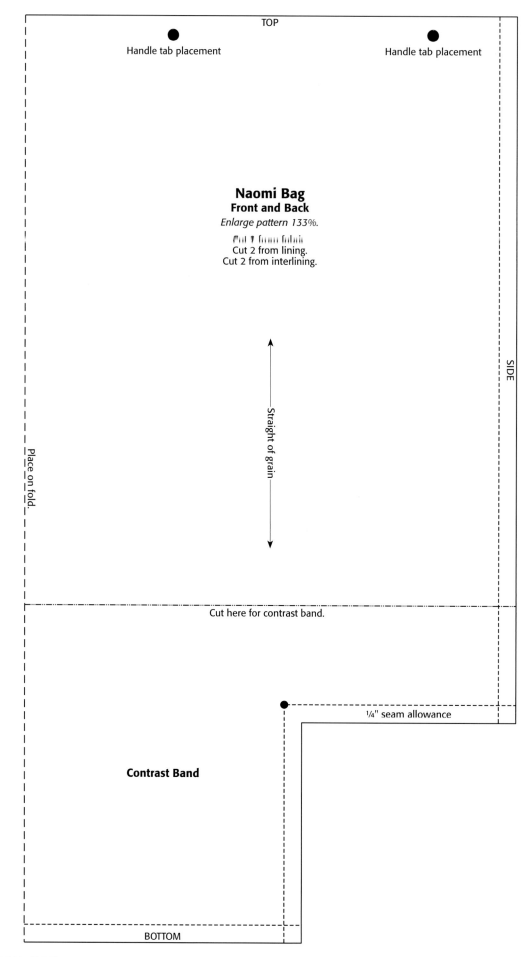

TOP

Handle tab placement

Handle tab placement

Naomi Bag
Front and Back
Enlarge pattern 133%.

Cut 1 from fabric.
Cut 2 from lining.
Cut 2 from interlining.

SIDE

Straight of grain

Place on fold.

Cut here for contrast band.

¼" seam allowance

Contrast Band

BOTTOM

DONNA BAG

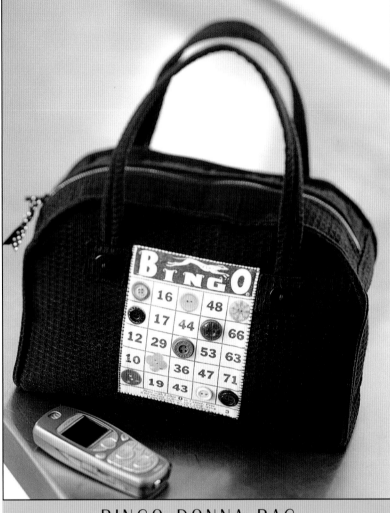

BINGO DONNA BAG

MATERIALS

The yardage is based on a 42" width. In addition to the items below, you'll need the general supplies listed on page 13.

- ¾ yard of black fabric for bag and handles
- ¾ yard of fabric for lining and pockets
- ¾ yard of interlining
- ⅛ yard of fusible fleece for handles
- Click-n-Craft Cotton Poplin fabric sheet
- Nonseparating zipper, 16"
- Decorative zipper pull
- 4 black buttons, ½" diameter, to place on tabs
- Assorted colorful buttons, ½" diameter, for bingo board
- 4 metal purse feet
- Heavyweight plastic needlepoint canvas
- Craft glue
- Serger (optional)
- Zipper foot

Secure your wallet, cell phone, and other can't-live-without items in this fun, practical purse. A zipper closure and metal feet create the look of miniature soft luggage. Sew this one on your serger! The bag measures 11¾" x 8", with a 4"-deep gusset.

CUTTING

See "Cutting and Marking" on page 14. Transfer the pattern markings to the fabric pieces before you begin sewing.

From the bag fabric, cut:

2 pieces using the front and back pattern (page 31)

2 pieces, 4⅝" x 7⅞", for side gussets

2 pieces, 2½" x 16", for top gussets

1 piece, 4" x 11½", for bottom

8 pieces, 2" x 2", for tabs

2 pieces, 3" x 18", for handles

From the interlining, cut:

2 pieces using the front and back pattern

2 pieces, 4⅝" x 7⅞", for side gussets

2 pieces, 2½" x 16", for top gussets

1 piece, 4" x 11½", for bottom

4 pieces, 2" x 2", for tabs

From the lining fabric, cut:

2 pieces using the front and back pattern

2 pieces, 4⅝" x 7⅞", for side gussets

2 pieces, 2½" x 16", for top gussets

2 pieces, 4" x 11½", for bottom insert

From the fusible fleece, cut:

2 strips, ¾" x 18", for handles

From the plastic canvas, cut:

1 piece, 3½" x 11", for bottom

ASSEMBLY

1. Fuse or baste each interlining piece to the wrong side of the corresponding fabric piece. (Four tab pieces will not have interlining.)

2. Place all the interlined pieces from step 1 (except the 2" x 2" tabs) on the lining pieces, wrong sides together. Serge the edges of each piece. If you do not have a serger, overcast the edges using a tight zigzag stitch.

3. Go to www.thevintageworkshop.com, click on Special Promotions, and enter PRS123 as your source code. Download the bingo card image. (Image is also available on the *Clothing Collage* Click-n-Craft CD-ROM from The Vintage Workshop.) Print the bingo image onto a Click-n-Craft Cotton Poplin sheet. Place the bingo card on the bag front, 1½" from the top and centered side to side. Sew around the edges using a decorative machine stitch. (See "Printing an Image" on page 6.)

4. Sew assorted ½" buttons to selected squares in the bingo board.

5. Unzip the zipper. Center the edge of the zipper tape on a long edge of a top gusset piece, right sides together. Using a zipper foot, stitch ¼" from the edge. Join the other top gusset piece to the zipper in the same way. Close the zipper. Trim the short ends of the zipper tape even with the ends of the gussets.

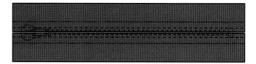

6. Pin a side gusset piece to one end of the zipper unit, right sides together. Stitch with a ⅝" seam allowance; be careful when stitching over the zipper teeth. Press the seam allowance away from the zipper. Topstitch the side gusset ¼" from the seam. Join the remaining side gusset to the opposite end of the zipper unit in the same way. Mark the midpoint of each long edge of the zipper/gusset unit.

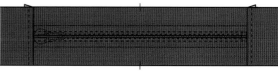

Midpoint

7. Use the handle pieces and the fusible-fleece strips to make two padded handles. Add three rows of stitching. (See "Making Shoulder Straps" on page 9.)

8. Layer a plain tab and an interlined tab right sides together. Stitch around the edges using a ¼" seam allowance. Trim the corners. Cut an X-shaped slit in one layer only. Turn right side out through this opening. Press. Make four tabs.

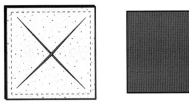

Make 4.

9. Place a tab, slit side down, on the bag front as marked. Pin. Slip one end of a handle between the tab and the bag. Topstitch around all four edges of the tab to secure the handle. Secure the other end of the handle to the bag front in the same way. Repeat for the bag back. Sew a button to the center of each tab through all layers.

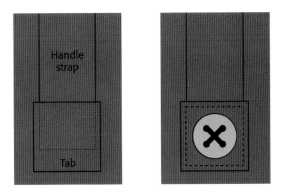

10. Pin the zipper unit to the top edge of the bag front, right sides together and matching the midpoints. Keep the handle free. Continue pinning down both sides of the bag front, clipping the bag seam allowance as needed to ease the fabric pieces together. Stitch using a ¼" seam allowance. On the right side, pinch the seam flat and topstitch close to the fold through all the layers. Repeat to join the bag back. Trim the gusset even with the lower edge of the bag front and back if the fit is not exact.

11. Open the zipper. Turn the bag wrong side out. Pin the bag bottom to the bag, right sides together and raw edges aligned. Stitch the short ends of the bag bottom to the side gussets using a ¼" seam allowance and starting and stopping ¼" from the edges. Next stitch the long edges to the bag front and bag back in the same way. Turn. Pinch and topstitch the seams as in step 10.

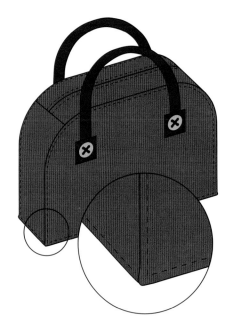

12. Turn the bag upside down. Measure in ¾" diagonally from each corner and make a mark. Using very sharp, small scissors, cut a small slit at each mark. Insert the prongs of the purse feet into the slits from the outside of the bag. Bend back the prongs on the inside of the bag with your fingers to hold the feet in place.

13. Place the plastic canvas piece in the bottom of the bag to test the fit. Trim if needed. Layer the bottom insert lining pieces right sides together. Stitch around three sides using a ¼" seam allowance. Turn right side out. Press. Insert the plastic canvas and slip-stitch the opening closed. Tack the insert to the bottom of the bag.

14. Add a decorative pull to the zipper so that it will be easy to open and close.

Plaid Donna Bag

Mix it up with two different plaids. For even more quirky fun, dip into your stash and cut each piece from a different fabric. Four 1" D rings anchor the strap handles. Omit the Click-n-Craft Cotton Poplin fabric sheet, buttons, and craft glue from the materials list. Follow "Cutting" on page 28, with the following changes:

- Cut the bag front, bag back, and bottom from a large-scale plaid.

- Cut the side and top gussets from a small-scale plaid.

- Omit the tabs.

- Omit the 3" x 18" fabric strips and the ¾" x 18" fusible-fleece strips for the handles. Instead, cut two strips, 3" x 42", from a small-scale plaid and two strips, ¾" x 42", from fusible fleece for the handles.

1. Complete "Assembly" steps 1–2 on page 28. Then skip to steps 5–6.

2. Use the plaid handle pieces and the fusible-fleece strips to make two padded handles. Add three rows of stitching. (See "Making Shoulder Straps" on page 9.)

3. Press a ½" fold at the end of a handle strap, slip on a D ring, and stitch closed. Place the D ring on the bag front, letting the strap hang off the lower edge. Topstitch each long edge of the strap to the purse. Topstitch across the strap, ½" below the D ring, and also along the opposite edge. Cut the excess strap even with the bottom edge of the bag. Repeat, using the same strap, to attach another D ring to the bag front. Repeat for the bag back using the same strap.

4. Cut the second handle strap into two 22" lengths. Press a ½" fold at each end. Slip each end around the top of a D ring and stitch closed.

5. Follow "Assembly" steps 10–14 to complete the bag.

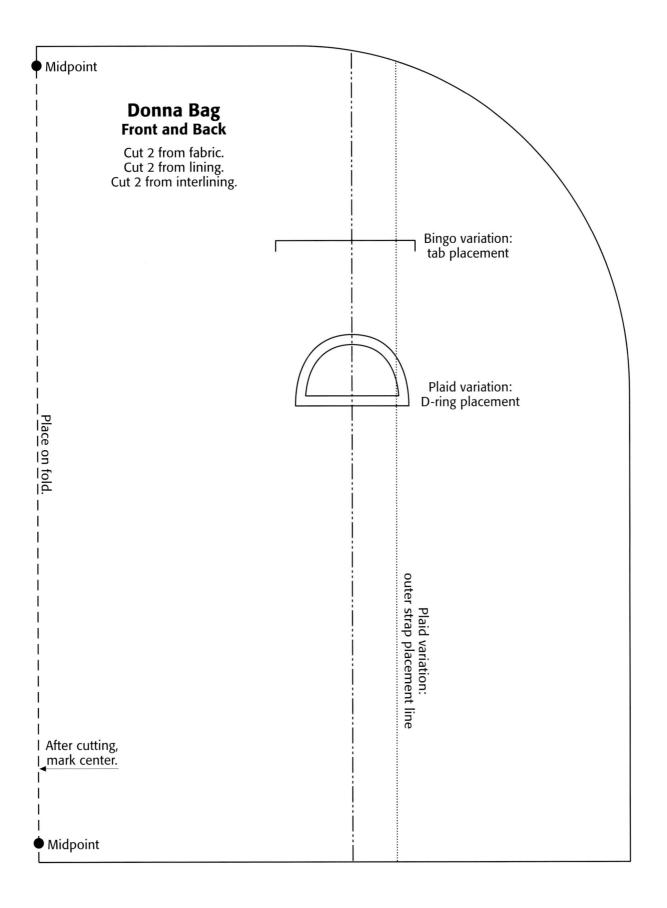

● Midpoint

Donna Bag
Front and Back

Cut 2 from fabric.
Cut 2 from lining.
Cut 2 from interlining.

Bingo variation:
tab placement

Plaid variation:
D-ring placement

Place on fold.

Plaid variation:
outer strap placement line

After cutting,
mark center.

● Midpoint

LARGE REBECCA BAG

LARGE REBECCA BAG

The large version of the Rebecca Bag makes a perfect diaper bag and carryall. Outside pockets hold baby bottles and wipes, and there's plenty of room for mommy and daddy essentials, too. The side pockets will be easier to sew if you use the free-arm feature of your sewing machine. The bag measures 20¾" x 16¾" x 3⅝" deep.

MATERIALS

The yardage is based on a 42" width. In addition to the items below, you'll need the general supplies listed on page 13.

- 1⅜ yards of fabric for bag, flap, strap, and pockets
- 1⅜ yards of lining
- 1⅜ yards of interlining
- Magnetic snap closure
- Sewing machine with free-arm feature

CUTTING

See "Cutting and Marking" on page 14. Transfer the pattern markings to the fabric pieces before you begin sewing.

From the bag fabric, cut:

2 pieces using the front and back pattern (page 35)

1 piece using the strap pattern (page 36)

1 piece using the flap pattern (page 37)

1 piece, 8¼" x 16", for front pocket

2 pieces using the side pocket pattern (page 38)

From the interlining, cut:

2 pieces using the front and back pattern

1 piece using the strap pattern

1 piece using the flap pattern

1 piece, 8¼" x 16", for front pocket

From the lining fabric, cut:

2 pieces using the front and back pattern

1 piece using the strap pattern

1 piece using the flap pattern

1 piece, 9⅜" x 16", for front pocket

ASSEMBLY

1. Fuse or baste each interlining piece to the wrong side of the corresponding fabric piece. (The side pocket pieces are not interlined.)

2. Layer the front pocket and the front pocket lining right sides together so that the lining extends 1⅛" beyond one long edge. Stitch around the other three sides using a ¼" seam allowance. Clip the corners. Turn and press. Fold and press the excess lining ½" toward the pocket. Repeat, so that the lining forms a double-fold band across the top of the pocket. Topstitch the lower edge of the band.

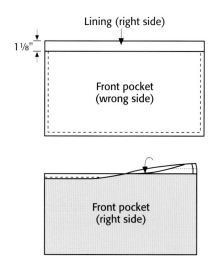

Lining (right side)

1⅛"

Front pocket
(wrong side)

Front pocket
(right side)

3. Center the pocket on the placement line on the bag front, right side up. Baste the side and bottom edges. Stitch one or more vertical lines through all layers to divide the pocket into compartments.

4. Serge or zigzag the raw edges of one side pocket piece. Fold down the top edge 2¾", right sides together, and stitch the side edges using a ¼" seam allowance. Turn right side out and press. Press the side and lower

edges ¼" to the wrong side. At one lower corner, fold the pocket right sides together, matching the dots. Stitch from dot to dot to box the corner. Repeat. Press the horizontal and vertical pocket creases. Stitch ⅛" from the fold to set each crease. Make two side pockets.

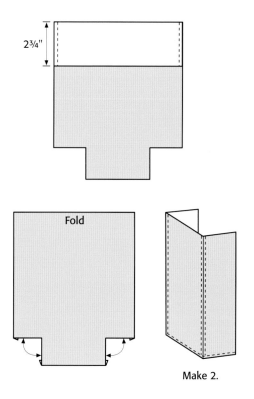

2¾"

Fold

Make 2.

5. Layer the bag front and bag back right sides together. Stitch *one* side seam only, using a ⅝" seam allowance. Press open. Center a side pocket on the seam, even with the lower edge of the *front* pocket. Pin. Topstitch the side and bottom edges of the pocket using the free-arm feature of your sewing machine. Repeat to add the second side pocket.

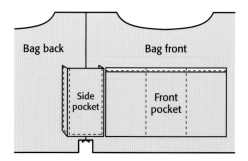

Bag back

Bag front

Side
pocket

Front
pocket

6. Stitch the bag bottom seam. Press open. To form the bottom corners, refold the bag, wrong side out, aligning a side seam on the bottom seam. Stitch from dot to dot to box the corner. Repeat to box the other corner.

7. Add a pocket to one or both bag linings if desired. (See "Inside Pockets" on page 12.) Add a magnetic snap closure to the linings. (See "Inserting Magnetic Snaps" on page 8.) Layer the bag linings, right sides together. Sew the side edges using a ⅝" seam allowance. Press open. Sew the bottom edges, leaving 6" open for turning. Press open. Box the lining corners as in step 6.

8. Layer the interlined strap and the strap lining right sides together. Stitch the long edges using a ⅜" seam allowance. Leave the short ends open. Trim the interlining close to the stitching. Turn and press. Baste the raw edges together.

9. Center one end of the strap on the bag side seam, right sides together and raw edges aligned. Baste the raw edges. Repeat, being careful not to twist the strap.

10. Layer the interlined flap piece and the flap lining piece right sides together. Stitch around three sides using a ¼" seam allowance and leaving one narrow end open. Clip the corners. Turn and press. Baste the raw edges to the bag. Pin the flap to the bag back, right sides together, between the dots. Baste.

11. Add a plastic canvas insert to the bottom of the bag. (See "Bottom Inserts" on page 13.) Join and tack the lining to the bag. (See "Joining the Lining" on page 15 and "Final Tacking" on page 15.)

Designer Flap

Use your computer, inkjet printer, and a free image download to add a special design to the bag flap. (Image is also available on *The Little Ones* Click-n-Craft CD-ROM from The Vintage Workshop.) Follow "Cutting" on page 32, with the following changes:

▪ Omit the flap piece cut from the bag fabric.

▪ Omit the flap interlining piece. Instead, cut one flap piece from fusible fleece.

1. Follow "Assembly" steps 1–9 on page 33.

2. Download the reading child image (go to www.thevintageworkshop.com, click on Special Promotions, and enter PRS123 as your source code) or select it from *The Little Ones* CD. Print the image onto a Click-n-Craft Cotton Poplin sheet. (See "Printing an Image" on page 6.)

3. Use the flap pattern to cut one flap from the printed sheet. Fuse the fleece to the wrong side of the flap. Use cotton quilting thread to machine quilt a diagonal pattern on the flap.

4. Follow "Assembly" steps 10 and 11 to complete the bag.

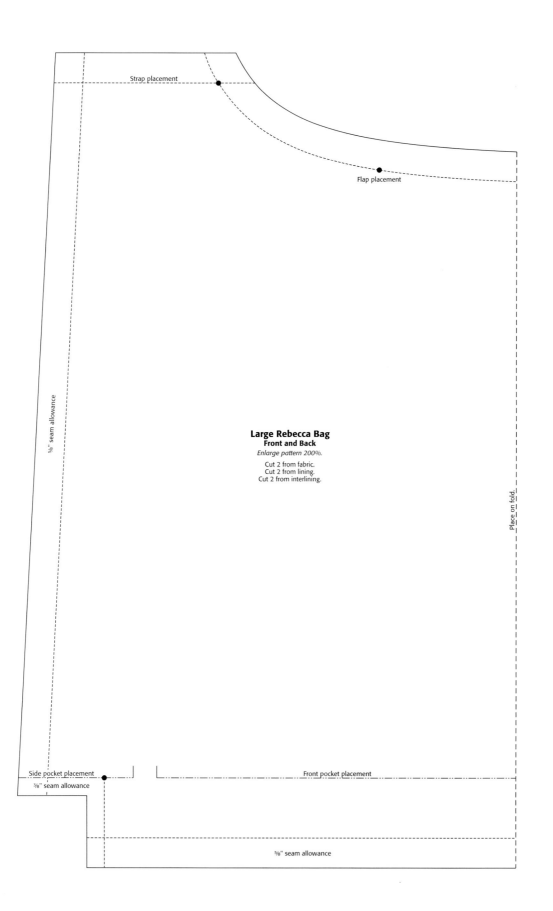

Strap placement

Flap placement

⅝" seam allowance

Large Rebecca Bag
Front and Back
Enlarge pattern 200%.

Cut 2 from fabric.
Cut 2 from lining.
Cut 2 from interlining.

Place on fold.

Side pocket placement

⅜" seam allowance

Front pocket placement

⅝" seam allowance

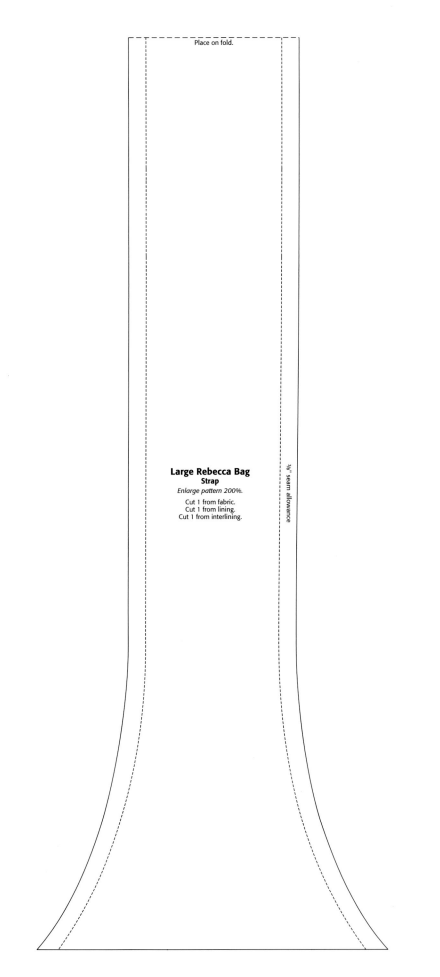

Place on fold.

Large Rebecca Bag
Strap
Enlarge pattern 200%.

Cut 1 from fabric.
Cut 1 from lining.
Cut 1 from interlining.

³⁄₈" seam allowance

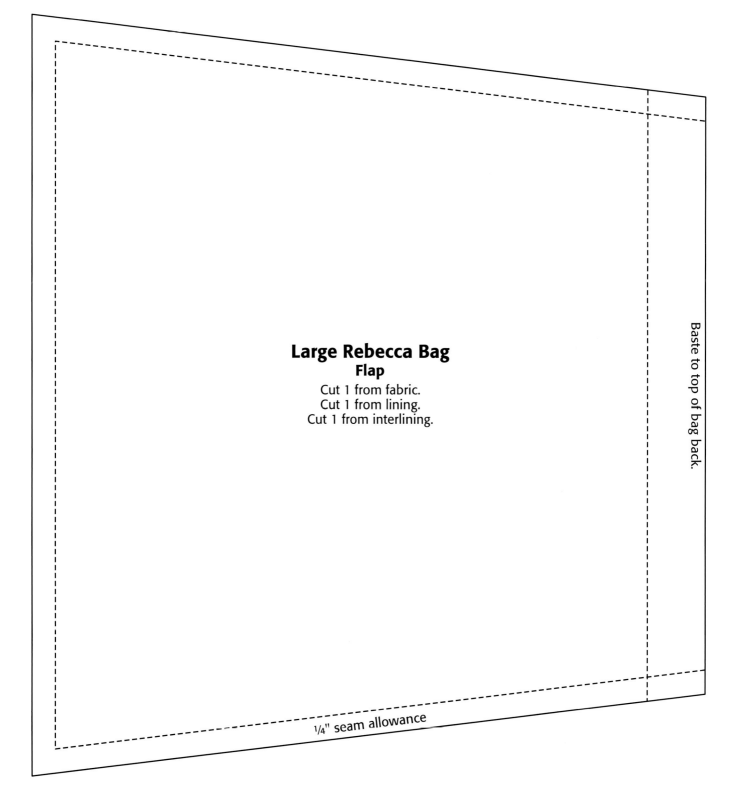

Large Rebecca Bag
Flap
Cut 1 from fabric.
Cut 1 from lining.
Cut 1 from interlining.

1/4" seam allowance

Baste to top of bag back.

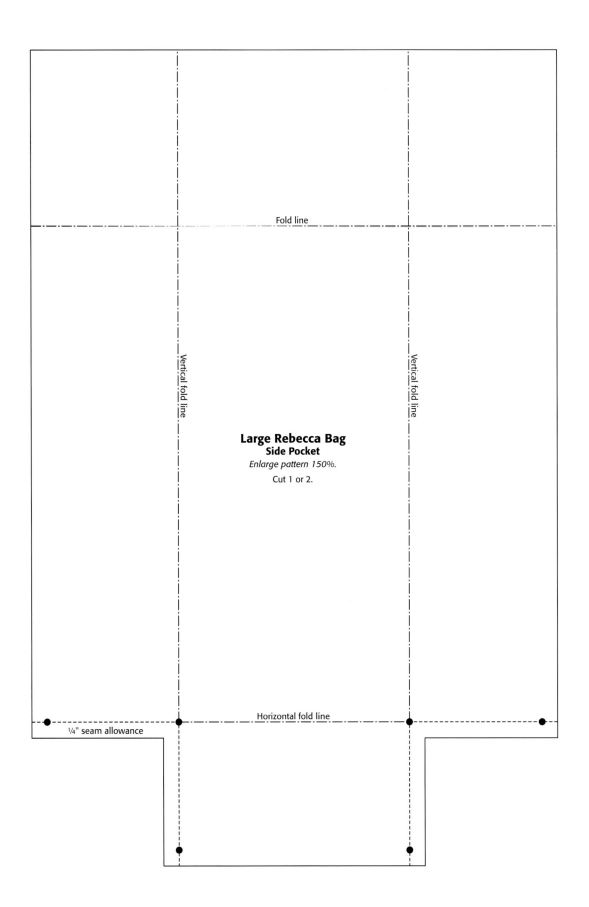

Fold line

Vertical fold line

Vertical fold line

Large Rebecca Bag
Side Pocket
Enlarge pattern 150%.
Cut 1 or 2.

Horizontal fold line

¼" seam allowance

SMALL REBECCA BAG

SMALL REBECCA BAG

The Small Rebecca Bag, 15¾" x 11¾" x 3" deep, is perfect for day trips when you're taking along snacks and picking up souvenirs.

MATERIALS

The yardage is based on a 42" width. In addition to the items below, you'll need the general supplies listed on page 13.

- ⅝ yard or 1⅛ yards* of fabric for bag and strap
- ⅝ yard of fabric for lining and pockets
- ⅝ yard of interlining
- 4" x 4" piece of fabric for covered button
- 2½" button to cover
- Magnetic snap closure (optional)
- Heavyweight plastic needlepoint canvas

*Choose the longer yardage to cut the pieces on the lengthwise grain.

CUTTING

See "Cutting and Marking" on page 14. Transfer the pattern markings to the fabric pieces before you begin sewing.

From the bag fabric, cut:

2 pieces using the front and back pattern (page 41)

1 piece using the strap pattern (page 41)

2 pieces using the flap pattern (page 42)

From the interlining, cut:

2 pieces using the front and back pattern

1 piece using the strap pattern

1 piece using the flap pattern

From the lining fabric, cut:

2 pieces using the front and back pattern

1 piece using the strap pattern

ASSEMBLY

1. Fuse or baste each interlining piece to the wrong side of the corresponding fabric piece. (One flap piece will not have interlining.)

2. Layer the interlined bag pieces right sides together. Stitch the side and bottom edges using a ⅝" seam allowance. Do not stitch the cutout corners. Press the seams open. If you basted the interlining in step 1, trim it close to the stitching line to reduce bulk in the seam allowance.

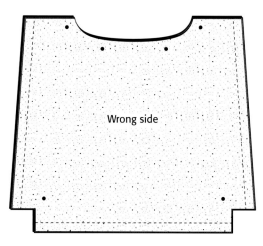

Wrong side

3. To form the bottom corners, open and refold the bag, right sides together, aligning a side seam on the bottom seam. Stitch the raw edges from dot to dot using a ⅝" seam allowance. Repeat to box the other corner. Turn the bag right side out. Press.

Fold   Fold

4. Add a pocket to one or both bag linings if desired. (See "Inside Pockets" on page 12.) Add a magnetic snap closure to the lining if desired. (See "Inserting Magnetic Snaps" on page 8.) Join the bag linings as in step 2, leaving 6" open in the bottom seam for turning. Sew the lining corners as in step 3.

5. Layer the interlined strap and the strap lining right sides together. Stitch the long edges using a ⅜" seam allowance. Leave the short ends open. Trim the interlining close to the seam. Turn and press. Baste the raw edges.

6. Center one end of the strap on the bag side seam between the dots, right sides together and raw edges aligned. Baste the raw edges. Repeat on the other side, being careful not to twist the strap.

7. Layer the plain flap and the interlined flap right sides together. Stitch around three sides using a ¼" seam allowance; leave the narrow end open. Clip the corners. Turn and press. Baste the raw edges.

8. Cover the button with fabric, following the manufacturer's package instructions. Stitch a vertical buttonhole in the flap, sizing it to fit your button. Center the flap on the bag back, right sides together and raw edges aligned. Baste.

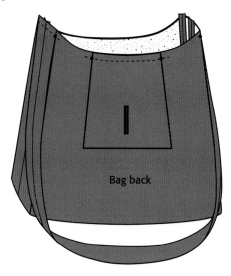

Bag back

9. Add a plastic canvas insert to the bottom of the bag (see "Bottom Inserts" on page 13). Join and tack the lining. (See "Joining the Lining" on page 15 and "Final Tacking" on page 15.) Sew the covered button to the front of the bag beneath the flap.

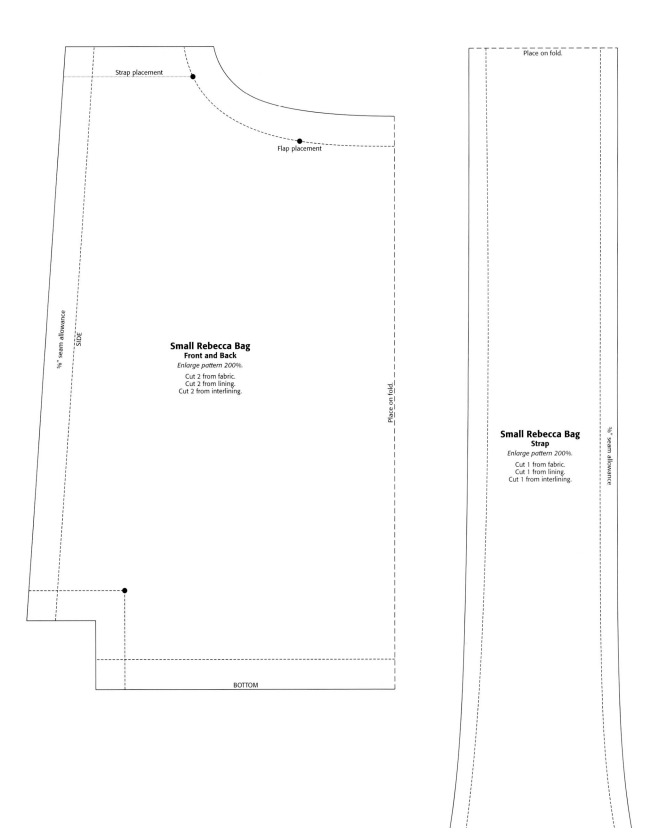

Strap placement

Flap placement

5/8" seam allowance

SIDE

Small Rebecca Bag
Front and Back
Enlarge pattern 200%.

Cut 2 from fabric.
Cut 2 from lining.
Cut 2 from interlining.

Place on fold.

BOTTOM

Place on fold.

Small Rebecca Bag
Strap
Enlarge pattern 200%.

Cut 1 from fabric.
Cut 1 from lining.
Cut 1 from interlining.

5/8" seam allowance

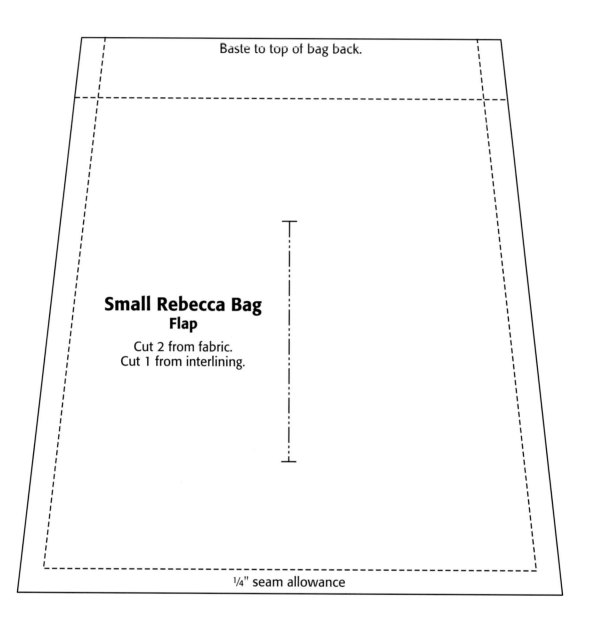

Baste to top of bag back.

Small Rebecca Bag
Flap

Cut 2 from fabric.
Cut 1 from interlining.

¼" seam allowance

HOBO BAG

PINK FLOWER HOBO BAG

YELLOW FLOWER HOBO BAG

This sturdy bag and its flower trim are made of wool felt. Just cut and sew—there's no need to serge or finish the edges. Choose a dark color, such as aubergine or cranberry red, for the bag. Choose bright colors, such as pink or yellow, for the flowers. The bag measures 14½" x 8" plus the handle length and is 7¼" deep.

MATERIALS

The yardage is based on a 42" width. In addition to the items below, you'll need the general supplies listed on page 13.

- ⅝ yard of wool felt for bag
- ⅛ yard of wool felt for lining, plus extra for pockets
- Scraps of wool felt for flower petals and flower center
- Scraps of green wool felt for leaves
- ⅝ yard of interlining
- Button for flower center
- Magnetic snap closure (optional)
- Heavyweight plastic needlepoint canvas

CUTTING

See "Cutting and Marking" on page 14. Transfer the pattern markings to the fabric pieces before you begin sewing. On the bag bottom and the bag bottom lining, mark the midpoint of each 7¾" edge.

From the wool felt for the bag, cut:
2 pieces using the front and back pattern (page 47)
1 piece, 7¾" x 8", for bag bottom

From the interlining, cut:
2 pieces using the front and back pattern
1 piece, 7½" x 7¾", for bag bottom

From the wool felt for the lining, cut:
2 pieces using the front and back pattern
1 piece, 7¾" x 8", for bag bottom

From the scraps of wool felt for the flower, cut:
4 pieces using the large petal pattern (page 48)
4 pieces using the small petal pattern (page 48)
1 piece using the flower-center pattern, fringing the edges as marked on the pattern (page 48)

From the green wool felt, cut:
1 piece using the flower-base pattern (page 48)
4 pieces using the leaf pattern (page 48)

ASSEMBLY

1. Fuse or baste each interlining piece to the wrong side of the corresponding bag piece. Note that the bag bottom interlining is cut slightly smaller than the bag bottom to allow a ⅛" margin all around.

2. Fold the bag front in half, right sides together. Stitch the strap ends together using a ¼" seam allowance. Press open. Repeat for the bag back.

3. Layer the bag front and bag back, right sides together. Stitch the side seams using a ½" seam allowance. Press open.

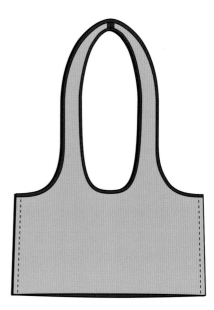

4. Pin the bag bottom piece to the bottom edges of the bag, right sides together, matching the midpoints on the bottom piece to the side seams on the bag. Stitch each edge with a ¼" seam allowance, easing around the corners.

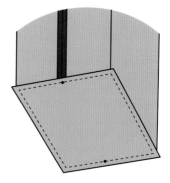

5. Add a pocket to one or both bag linings if desired. (See "Inside Pockets" on page 12.) Add a magnetic snap closure to the lining if desired. (See "Inserting Magnetic Snaps" on page 8.) Sew the bag lining pieces together as in steps 2–4.

6. Add a plastic canvas insert to the bottom of the bag (see "Bottom Inserts" on page 13).

7. Turn the bag right side out. Insert the lining, wrong side out, into the bag. Pin the straps and upper edges together. Topstitch ¼" from the raw edges with contrasting thread. Tack the lining. (See "Final Tacking" on page 15.)

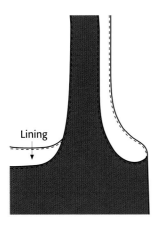

Lining

8. Arrange the leaves on the flower base and tack in place. Add the large petals, small petals, and flower center, tacking after each addition, to create a flower. Tack the flower to the bag near the top edge.

9. Sew a button to the flower center.

Pom-Pom Hobo Bag

A longer strap makes it extra-easy to sling this bag over your shoulder. Finish with two yards of pom-pom trim. Follow "Cutting" on page 44, adding the strap-extension pattern (page 46) to the bag front and back pattern. Instead of wool felt, use ⅞ yard each of two decorator fabrics (for the bag exterior and lining), and omit the flower.

1. Complete "Assembly" steps 1–2 on page 44.

2. Layer the bag front and bag back right sides together. Stitch one side seam using a ½" seam allowance. Press open. Lay the bag flat, right side up. Pin the trim across the joined front and back pieces, so the pom-poms dangle about 1" above the bottom edge. Stitch. Cut off the excess even with the side edge of the bag. Add 3 more rows of pom-pom trim, letting them overlap slightly.

3. Sew the remaining side seam. Press open. Press the curved raw edges ¼" to the wrong side.

4. Follow "Assembly" steps 4–7 to complete the bag.

3. Layer the bag front and back right sides together. Stitch one side seam using a ½" seam allowance. Press open. Center the side pocket on the seam, 1⅝" from the lower edge. Topstitch the side and bottom edges.

4. Sew the remaining bag side seam. Press open. Press the curved raw edges of the straps ¼" to the wrong side.

5. Follow "Assembly" steps 4–7 to complete the bag.

At-the-Office Hobo Bag

For this version of the bag, use ⅞ yard each of two cotton prints (for the bag exterior and lining), and omit the flower. Follow "Cutting" on page 44, adding the strap-extension pattern (right) to the bag front and back pattern. Then, from the bag fabric, cut one side pocket pattern (page 49). Omit the flower.

1. Complete "Assembly" steps 1–2 on page 44.

2. Serge or zigzag the raw edges of the pocket. Fold down the top edge 2⅛", wrong side out. Stitch the side edges using a ¼" seam allowance. Turn right side out and press. Press the side and lower edges ¼" to the wrong side. At one lower corner, fold the pocket wrong side out, matching the dots. Stitch from dot to dot to box the corner. Repeat. Press the horizontal and vertical creases. Stitch ⅛" from the fold to set each crease. (For an illustration of side pocket construction, see the Large Rebecca Bag, step 4, on page 33.)

Hobo Bag
Strap Extension
Enlarge pattern 167%.

Tape this end to front and back pattern, overlapping ¼".

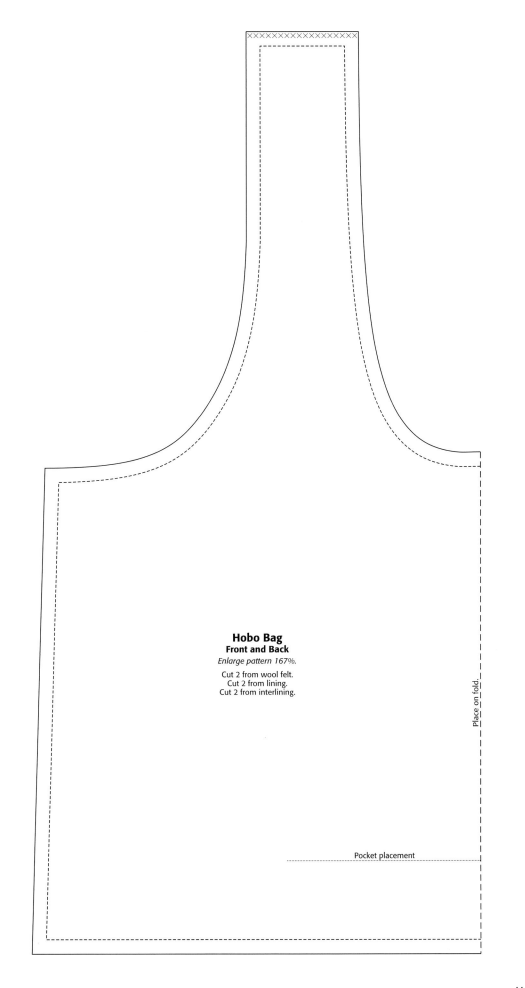

Hobo Bag
Front and Back

Enlarge pattern 167%.

Cut 2 from wool felt.
Cut 2 from lining.
Cut 2 from interlining.

Place on fold.

Pocket placement

Hobo Bag Patterns

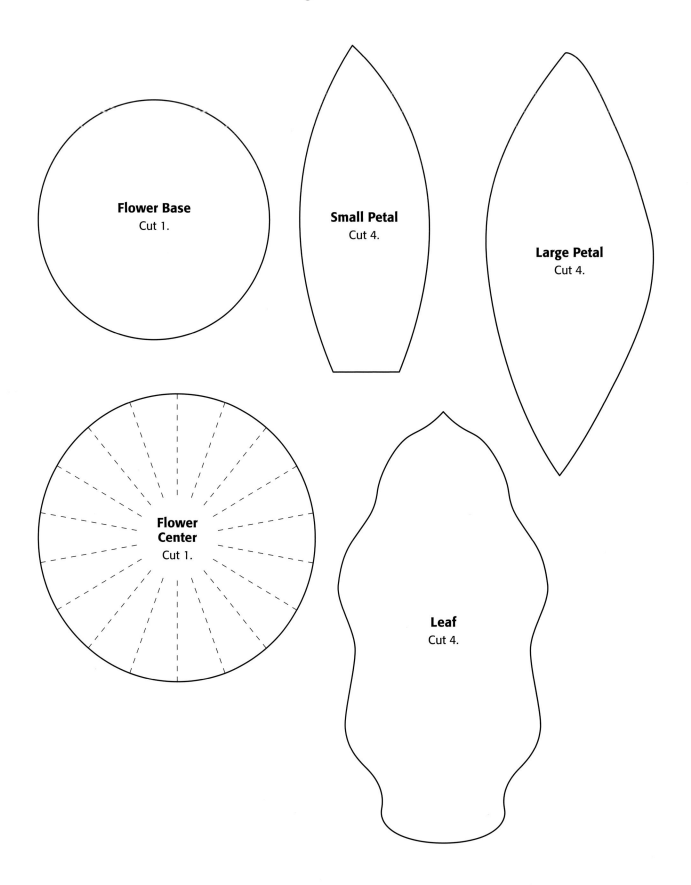

Flower Base
Cut 1.

Small Petal
Cut 4.

Large Petal
Cut 4.

Flower Center
Cut 1.

Leaf
Cut 4.

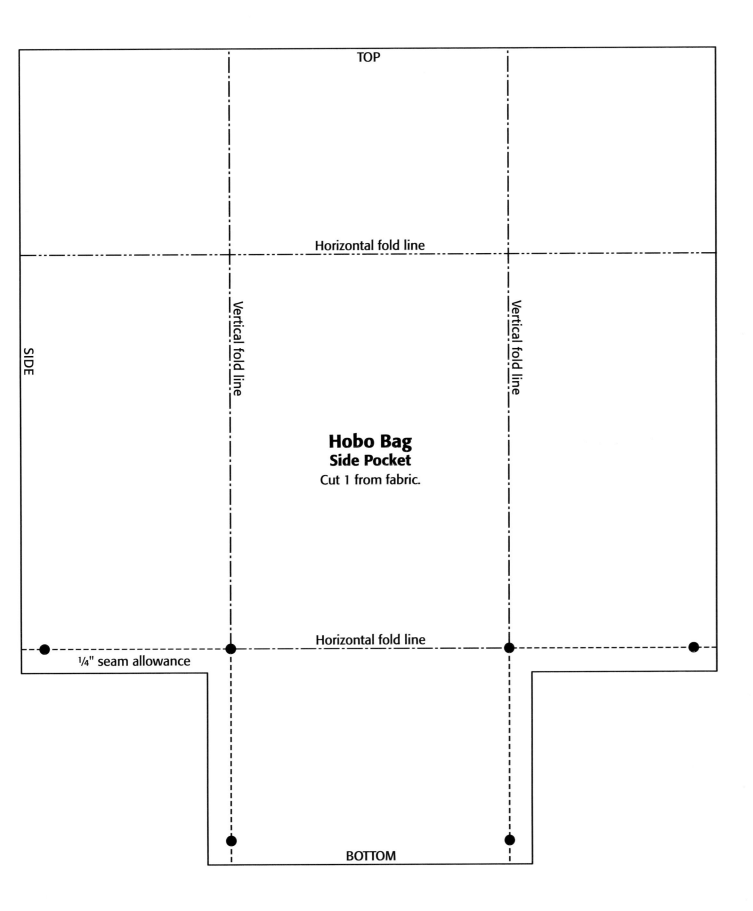

TOP

Horizontal fold line

Vertical fold line

Vertical fold line

SIDE

Hobo Bag
Side Pocket
Cut 1 from fabric.

Horizontal fold line

¼" seam allowance

BOTTOM

RACHEL BAG

BLUE WILLOW RACHEL BAG
BARK CLOTH RACHEL BAG

Use the instructions that follow to make the Blue Willow Rachel Bag. For directions on making the Bark Cloth variation, see page 52.

MATERIALS

The yardage is based on a 42" width. In addition to the items below, you'll need the general supplies listed on page 13.

- ¾ yard of fabric for bag
- ¾ yard of fabric for lining
- ¾ yard of interlining
- Corded button, 2" diameter, with tassels
- Purchased handle
- 12" zipper
- Snap
- Heavyweight plastic needlepoint canvas
- Serger (optional)
- Zipper foot

CUTTING

See "Cutting and Marking" on page 14. Transfer the pattern markings to the fabric pieces before you begin sewing.

From the bag fabric, cut:

1 piece using the front pattern (page 53)

2 pieces using the back pattern (page 53)

1 piece using the bottom pattern (page 54)

The Rachel Bag's A-line silhouette draws attention to the faux flap closure and round purchased handle. Access to this roomy bag is actually through a zippered opening in the back. The bag measures 12" x 15" plus handle and is 3¼" deep.

From the interlining, cut:

1 piece using the front pattern

2 pieces using the back pattern

1 piece using the bottom pattern

From the lining fabric, cut:

1 piece using the front pattern

2 pieces using the back pattern

1 piece using the bottom pattern

ASSEMBLY

1. Fuse or baste each interlining piece to the wrong side of the corresponding bag piece.

2. Layer the interlined bag front and the corresponding lining piece wrong sides together. Baste close to the edge all around. Serge or zigzag the edges for a clean finish. Line the bag back pieces and the bag bottom piece in the same way.

3. Layer the bag back pieces right sides together. Starting at one edge, stitch the center back seam with a ⅝" seam allowance. When you reach the first dot, stop, backstitch, and reset the machine to the longest stitch length. Machine baste to ½" beyond the next dot, stop, backstitch to the dot, and reset the machine for a regular stitch length. Sew the remainder of the seam. Press the seam allowance open.

4. Center the zipper facedown on the seam between the dots with the top of zipper toward the narrow end of the bag. Hand baste. Using a zipper foot, stitch the zipper from the right side. Use a seam ripper to pick out the hand and machine basting. Open the zipper.

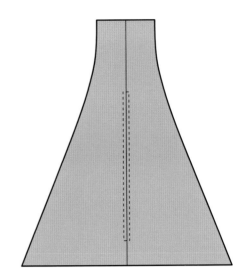

5. Layer the bag front and bag back pieces right sides together. Stitch the side and top edges using a ¼" seam allowance. Leave the bottom open.

6. Pin the bag bottom piece to the bag, right sides together and dots matching the bag side seams. Stitch using a ¼" seam allowance. Add the plastic canvas insert to the bottom of the bag. (See "Bottom Inserts" on page 13.) Turn right side out through the zipper opening.

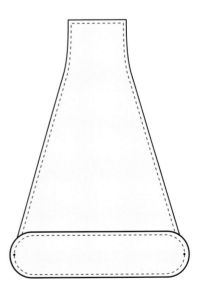

7. Fold down the top of the bag, forming a 5"-long flap on the bag front. Sew a button to the outside of the flap, centering it on the seam. Sew a snap to the underside to secure the flap to the bag. Open the flap, slip it through a round handle, and snap closed.

Bark Cloth Rachel Bag

For a 1940s look, use retro bark cloth prints—one dark and one light. You'll also need a coordinating tweed for the back (which forms the flap). Accent your fabric finds with a jumbo rhinestone-studded button and a wooden bead handle. Follow "Cutting" on page 50, with the following changes:

- Cut all the lining and interlining pieces first.
- Cut two pieces from tweed using the bag back pattern.
- Trim off the lower edge of the bag front pattern. Use the modified pattern to cut one bag front from the dark bark cloth print. Cut one of the bottom band pattern (page 55) from the light print.
- Cut one bag bottom pattern from the light print.

1. Layer the bottom band piece and the bag front piece right sides together. Stitch using a ¼" seam allowance. Press open.

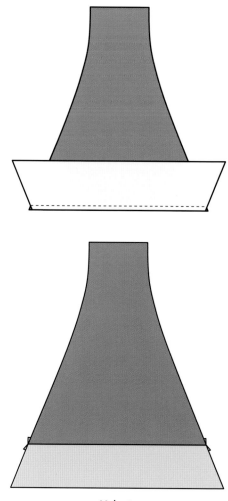

Make 1.

2. Follow "Assembly" steps 1–6 on page 51 using the new bag front.

3. Follow "Assembly" step 7 to make the flap. Sew a buttonhole in the flap. Sew a button to the bag front. Open the flap, slip the handle onto it, and button closed.

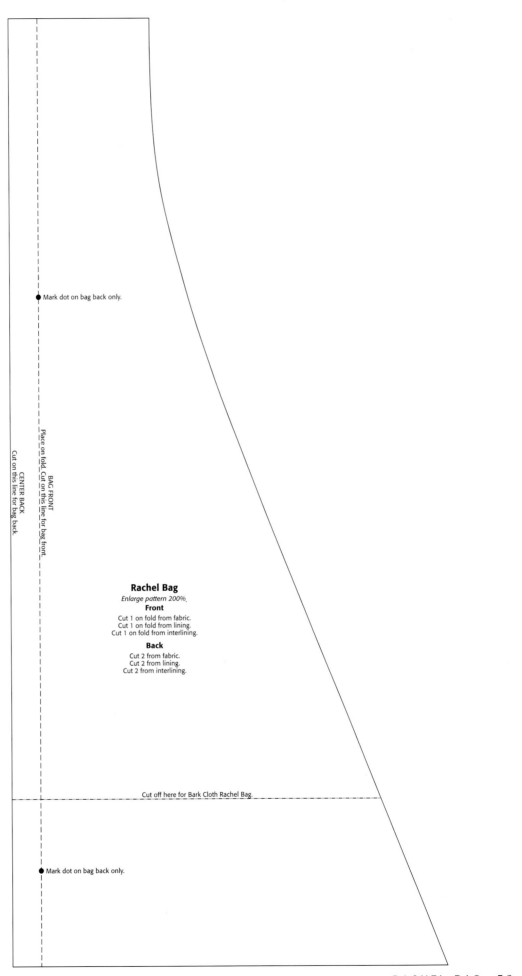

● Mark dot on bag back only.

Place on fold. Cut on this line for bag front.

BAG FRONT

CENTER BACK
Cut on this line for bag back.

Rachel Bag
Enlarge pattern 200%.
Front
Cut 1 on fold from fabric.
Cut 1 on fold from lining.
Cut 1 on fold from interlining.

Back
Cut 2 from fabric.
Cut 2 from lining.
Cut 2 from interlining.

Cut off here for Bark Cloth Rachel Bag.

● Mark dot on bag back only.

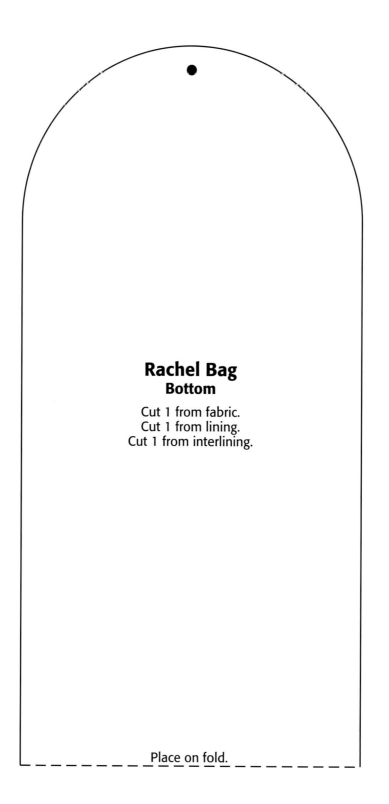

Rachel Bag
Bottom

Cut 1 from fabric.
Cut 1 from lining.
Cut 1 from interlining.

Place on fold.

Rachel Bag
Bottom Band

Cut 1 from fabric.

Place on fold.

PRETTY SNAPPY (LARGE BAG)

PRETTY SNAPPY (LARGE BAG)

MATERIALS

The yardage is based on a 42" width. In addition to the items below, you'll need the general supplies listed on page 13.

- ¾ yard or 1⅛ yards* of large-scale polka-dot fabric for bag and handles
- 4" x 16¼" piece of small-scale polka-dot fabric for front band
- ⅝ yard of windowpane-plaid fabric for lining and pockets
- ½ yard of interlining
- ⅛ yard of fusible fleece for handles
- 1 yard each of solid pink and dotted ribbon for center-band trim
- 1¼ yards of feather trim
- Heavyweight plastic needlepoint canvas
- Purchased 18" straight hex-open frame

*Choose the longer yardage to cut the pieces on the lengthwise grain.

The casing around the top edge of this bag conceals a spring-loaded metal frame. Coax the frame gently with your fingertips and it pops open into a wide hexagon, giving you access to the bag interior. Choose a fun fabric for the lining—it shows on the outside as the casing for the hardware. The bag measures 18" x 12" x 5" deep.

CUTTING

See "Cutting and Marking" on page 14. Transfer the pattern markings to the fabric pieces before you begin sewing.

From the large-scale polka dot, cut:
2 pieces using the front and back pattern (page 59)

2 pieces, 3" x 24", for handles

From the interlining, cut:
2 pieces using the front and back pattern

From the windowpane plaid, cut:
2 pieces using the front and back pattern

From the fusible fleece, cut:
4 pieces, ¾" x 24", for handles

ASSEMBLY

1. Fuse or baste each interlining piece to the wrong side of the corresponding fabric piece.

2. Press the long edges of the front band piece ¼" to the wrong side. Center the front band on the bag front. Topstitch each folded edge. Place a trim along each edge of the front band. Fuse or topstitch in place. Place a second trim next to the first trim, overlapping the edges slightly. Fuse or topstitch in place. Cut the ends of the trim even with the bag edges.

3. Layer the bag front and bag back pieces right sides together. Stitch the side seams from the dot to the lower edge using a ¼" seam allowance. Stitch the bottom edges. Do not stitch the cutout corners. Press all the seams open.

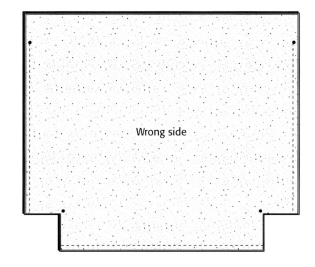

Wrong side

4. To form the bottom corners, refold the bag, right sides together, aligning a side seam on the bottom seam. Stitch the raw edges from dot to dot using a ¼" seam allowance. Repeat to box the other corner. Press.

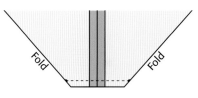

Fold · Fold

5. Add a pocket to one or both bag linings if desired. (See "Inside Pockets" on page 12.) Join the bag lining pieces as in step 3, leaving 4" open at the bottom seam for turning. Sew the lining corners as in step 4.

6. Add a plastic canvas insert to the bottom of the bag. (See "Bottom Inserts" on page 13.)

7. Insert the lining into the bag, right sides together. Match the side seams and raw edges, and pin. Sew across the entire top of the bag, pivoting at the corners and sewing into the V on each side. Use a ¼" seam allowance. Clip into the seam allowance at each dot. Clip the corners. Turn right side out and press.

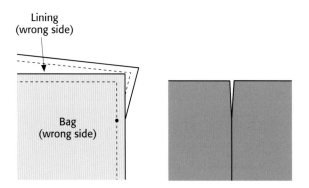

8. Close the opening and tack the lining to the bag. (See "Final Tacking" on page 15.) Fold down the top edge even with the dots so that the lining forms a 1"-wide contrasting band around the top of the bag. Topstitch the lower edge of the band to form a self-casing for the straight hex-open frame.

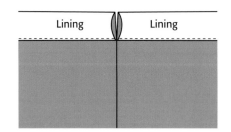

9. Use the fabric and fusible-fleece handle pieces to make two straps. (See "Making Shoulder Straps" on page 9.) Pin both raw edges of a strap slightly below the topstitched edge on the bag front as indicated on the pattern. Stitch in place over the topstitching. Repeat on the bag back.

10. Fuse or tack the feather trim around the top edge of the bag to conceal the topstitching. Be careful not to interfere with the casing. Add the hex-open frame to complete the bag. (See "Inserting a Metal Hex-Open Frame" on page 8.)

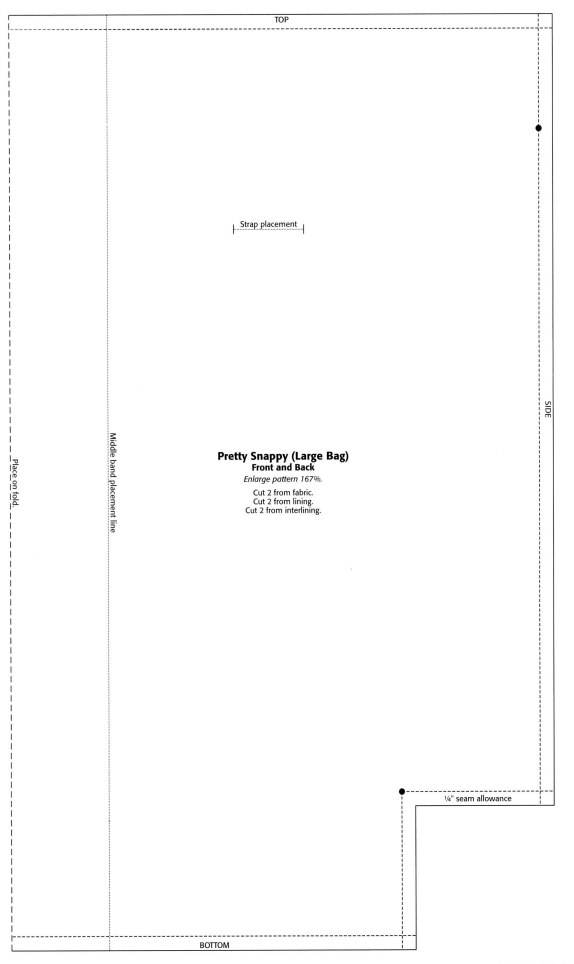

TOP

Strap placement

SIDE

Middle band placement line

Place on fold.

Pretty Snappy (Large Bag)
Front and Back
Enlarge pattern 167%.

Cut 2 from fabric.
Cut 2 from lining.
Cut 2 from interlining.

¼" seam allowance

BOTTOM

PRETTY SNAPPY (SMALL BAG)

PRETTY SNAPPY (SMALL BAG)

This smaller version of the Pretty Snappy Bag uses a 14" hex-open frame. The bag measures 14" x 9" x 4" deep.

MATERIALS

The yardage is based on a 42" width. In addition to the items below, you'll need the general supplies listed on page 13.

- ¾ yard or ⅞ yard* of pink print for bag and handles
- ½ yard of white polka-dot fabric for lining
- ½ yard of interlining

- ⅛ yard of fusible fleece for handles
- 1 yard each of black fringe and pink braid
- ⅔ yard of gingham ribbon for bow
- Heavyweight plastic needlepoint canvas
- Purchased 14" straight hex-open frame

Choose the longer yardage to cut the pieces on the lengthwise grain.

CUTTING

See "Cutting and Marking" on page 14. Transfer the pattern markings to the fabric pieces before you begin sewing.

From the bag fabric, cut:
2 pieces using the front and back pattern (page 61)
2 pieces, 3" x 24", for the straps

From the interlining, cut:
2 pieces using the front and back pattern

From the lining fabric, cut:
2 pieces using the front and back pattern

From the fusible fleece, cut:
4 pieces, ¾" x 24", for straps

ASSEMBLY

Follow the assembly instructions for the Pretty Snappy Large Bag (page 57). Omit step 2. In step 10, sew the trim around the lower edge of the casing. Tie the gingham ribbon into a bow and stitch it to the front of the bag.

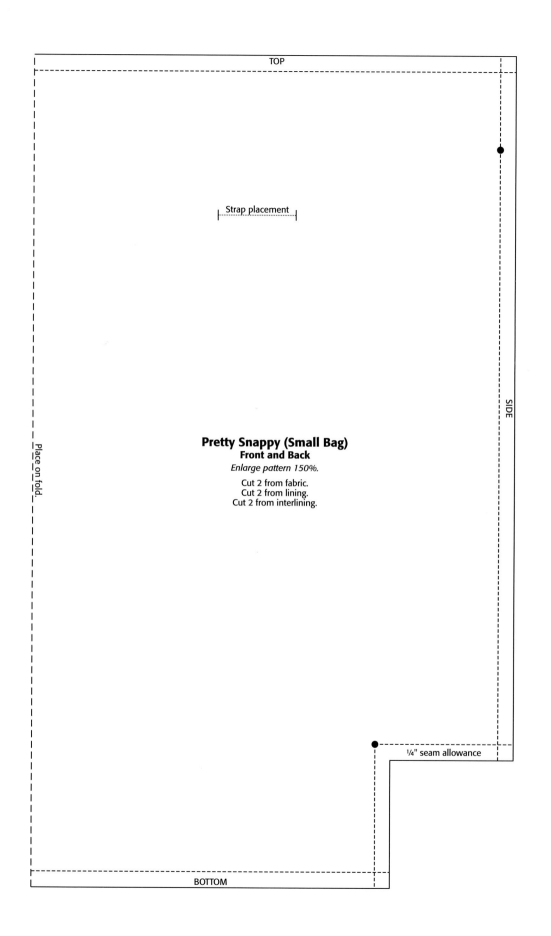

TOP

SIDE

Strap placement

Place on fold.

Pretty Snappy (Small Bag)
Front and Back
Enlarge pattern 150%.

Cut 2 from fabric.
Cut 2 from lining.
Cut 2 from interlining.

¼" seam allowance

BOTTOM

POCKETBOOK PURSE

**RICKRACK POCKETBOOK PURSE
PATCHES POCKETBOOK PURSE**

Dip into your stash to find the perfect coordinating fabrics for this sweet patchwork purse. The project variations let you show off your hand-appliqué and hand-quilting skills. Bias-cut trim and handles add a dressmaker's touch. Each bag measures 14" x 9" plus handles.

Use the instructions that follow to make the red Rickrack Pocketbook Purse. For directions on making the Patches variation, see page 65.

MATERIALS

The yardage is based on a 42" width. In addition to the items below, you'll need the general supplies listed on page 13.

- ½ yard of red gingham for bag, trim, and handles
- ¼ yard of red floral print for bag
- ¼ yard of small-scale red print for bag
- ⅛ yard or scraps of pink solid fabric for bag
- Scraps of assorted yellow and green fabrics for circles
- 1 yard of ¾"-wide white eyelet trim
- 1¼ yards of baby rickrack
- 2" x 2" scrap of fabric for covered button
- ⅜ yard of fabric for lining
- ⅜ yard of fusible fleece
- Magnetic snap closure (optional)
- Template plastic or cardboard

CUTTING

See "Cutting and Marking" on page 14. Transfer the pattern markings to the fabric pieces before you begin sewing.

From the red gingham, cut:

2 pieces, 3½" x 16½", for patchwork

3½"-wide bias strips; then piece together to make a 70"-long strip

From the red floral print, cut:

2 strips, 4" x 16½", for patchwork

From the pink solid, cut:

2 strips, 1¾" x 16½", for patchwork

From the small-scale red print, cut:

2 strips, 3¾" x 16½", for patchwork

From the yellow and green fabrics, cut:

16 pieces using the circle A pattern (page 67), for appliqués

From the lining fabric, cut:

2 pieces using the front and back pattern (page 66)

From the fusible fleece, cut:

2 pieces, 12" x 17", for patchwork backing

From the template plastic or cardboard, cut:

1 template using the circle B pattern (page 67)

ASSEMBLY

1. Layer a floral print piece and a gingham piece right sides together. Stitch one long edge using a ¼" seam allowance. Press the seam open. Join a pink piece to the gingham piece. Press. Join a red print piece to the

pink piece. Press. Make two. Fuse a piece of fleece to the wrong side of each patchwork piece.

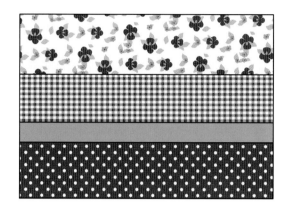

2. From each patchwork piece, cut one piece using the front and back pattern. Mark the tuck lines on the wrong side of each piece. Quilt the bag pieces by hand or machine.

3. Transfer the rickrack placement pattern (page 67) to the gingham section of the bag front. (See "Cutting and Marking" on page 14.) Pin rickrack along the placement line. Stitch. Repeat for the bag back.

4. Center the plastic circle template on the wrong side of a fabric circle. Press the edges of the fabric circle onto the template with a warm iron. Make 16.

5. Pin eight circles to the bag front, close to the rickrack, as shown below and in the project photograph (page 62). Hand appliqué each circle with matching thread. Repeat for the bag back.

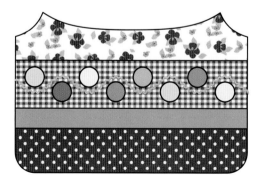

6. Fold each tuck, matching the dash lines. Baste across the top. Repeat.

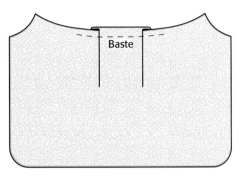

7. Layer the bag pieces right sides together. Stitch the side and bottom edges using a ¼" seam allowance. Press seams open. Turn right side out.

8. Make tucks in the bag lining pieces as in step 6. Add a magnetic snap closure to the lining if desired. (See "Inserting Magnetic Snaps" on page 8.) Sew together the bag lining pieces as in step 7, using a ⅜" seam allowance. Insert the lining into the bag, wrong sides together and seams aligned. Baste the raw edges.

9. Fold the bias strip lengthwise in half, wrong sides together. Pin the binding strip to the curved upper edge of the bag front, right sides together and raw edges aligned. Stitch using a ½" seam allowance. Trim off the excess binding. Fold the binding onto the lining, concealing the seam allowance. Slip-stitch the binding in place over the edge of the bag. Repeat for the bag back.

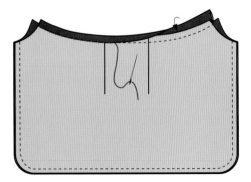

10. Starting ½" beyond a side seam, pin the remaining binding strip to the purse, right sides together and raw edges aligned. Beginning at the side seam, stitch for about 3" using a ½" seam allowance. At the top of the bag, stop and backstitch. Measure 18" of strip for the handle. Starting at the 18" mark, resume pinning the strip to the other end of the bag, taking care not to twist the handle. Stitch this section, backstitching at the beginning and end of the bag. Measure and mark off another 18" of strip for the second handle. Resume the pinning and stitching on the first side. When you reach the starting point, cut off the excess, fold in the end, and slip-stitch for a neat finish.

11. Fold the bias strip onto the lining side of the bag, concealing the seam allowance, and slip-stitch. Fold the loose 18" sections to make handles that are the same width as the binding. Pin. Topstitch each handle close to the edges, backstitching at the beginning and end where the handle meets the bag.

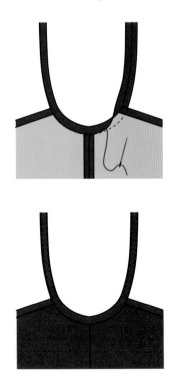

Patches Pocketbook Purse

Small bits of fabric tumble across the front of this soft quilted purse. Quilt by hand or machine. In addition to the materials listed below, you'll need a small button and 6" of cording for the button loop.

From a red print (¼ yard), cut:
2 pieces, 5¾" x 8½"

From a blue print (¼ yard), cut:
2 pieces, 5¾" x 8½"

From a cream fabric (⅜ yard), cut:
2 pieces, 8½" x 11"

From fusible fleece (⅜ yard), cut:
2 pieces, 12" x 17", for patchwork backing

From assorted prints and plaids, cut:
14 pieces, 1½" x 2"

From a plaid fabric (½ yard), cut:
3½"-wide bias strips; then piece together to make a 70"-long strip

From lining fabric (⅜ yard), cut:
2 pieces using the front and back pattern (page 66)

1. Layer a red 5¾" x 8½" piece and a blue 5¾" x 8½" piece right sides together. Stitch one long edge using a ¼" seam allowance. Press the seam open. Join a cream 8½" x 11" piece to the red/blue unit. Press. Make two. Fuse a piece of fleece to the wrong side of each patchwork piece.

Make 2.

2. From each patchwork piece, cut one piece using the front and back pattern. Mark the tuck lines on the wrong side of each piece.

3. Press the raw edges of each 1½" x 2" piece ¼" to the wrong side. Pin seven pieces to the cream section of the bag front, skewing them for a playful look. Hand appliqué each piece with matching thread. Hand quilt ¼" around the edges of the appliqués in contrasting thread. Quilt the red and blue sections as desired. Make two.

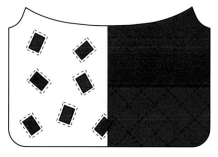

Make 2.

4. Follow "Assembly" steps 6–7 on page 64. Fold the button loop cord in half. Center the ends of the cord on the top raw edge of the bag back. Baste.

5. Follow "Assembly" steps 8–11. Sew the button to the front of the bag to complete the loop closure.

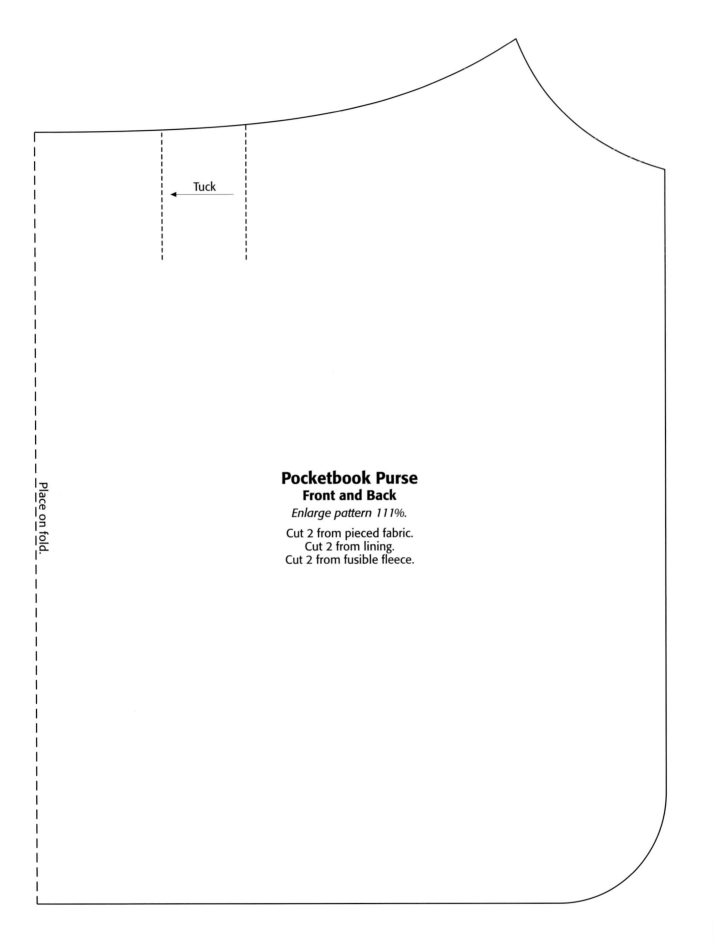

Tuck

Place on fold.

Pocketbook Purse
Front and Back
Enlarge pattern 111%.

Cut 2 from pieced fabric.
Cut 2 from lining.
Cut 2 from fusible fleece.

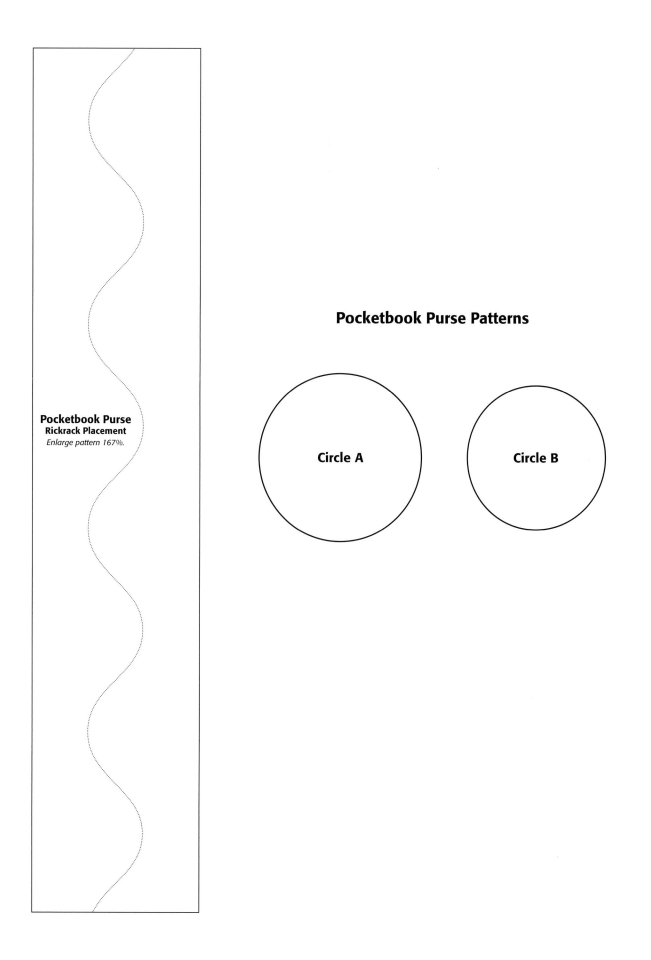

Pocketbook Purse
Rickrack Placement
Enlarge pattern 167%.

Pocketbook Purse Patterns

Circle A

Circle B

LARGE CARPETBAG

LARGE CARPETBAG

Whether you're traveling around the world or just to the supermarket, a carpetbag is a treat to use. Choose an exotic upholstery print for a vintage Victorian look, or go thoroughly modern with one of today's hot palettes. The lining fabric does double-duty in this bag; it folds to the outside to form a casing for the spring-loaded metal tubular frame. The bag measures 15" x 12" x 4" deep.

MATERIALS

The yardage is based on a 42" width. In addition to the items below, you'll need the general supplies listed on page 13.

- ½ yard of tapestry-print fabric for bag
- ½ yard of embroidered red silk for lining
- ⅜ yard or ¾ yard* of small-scale plaid for straps
- ½ yard of interlining
- ⅛ yard of fusible fleece for straps
- 2¼ yards of trim, ¾" wide
- Heavyweight plastic needlepoint canvas
- Purchased 12" tubular frame

*Choose the longer yardage to cut the pieces on the lengthwise grain.

CUTTING

See "Cutting and Marking" on page 14. Transfer the pattern markings to the fabric pieces before you begin sewing.

From the bag fabric, cut:
2 pieces using the front and back pattern (page 70)

From the interlining, cut:
2 pieces using the front and back pattern

From the lining fabric, cut:
2 pieces using the front and back pattern

From the strap fabric, cut:
2 pieces, 3½" x 20"

From the fusible fleece, cut:
2 pieces, 1¼" x 20", for straps

ASSEMBLY

1. Fuse or baste an interlining piece to the wrong side of each bag piece.

2. Layer the interlined front and back pieces right sides together. Starting at the dot, stitch down the side edges using a ¼" seam allowance. Stitch the bottom edges. Do not stitch the cutout corners. Press the seams open.

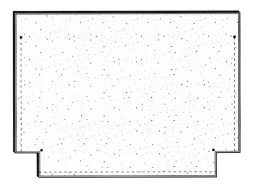

3. To form the bottom corners, refold the bag, right sides together, aligning a side seam on the bottom seam. Stitch the raw edges from dot to dot using a ¼" seam allowance. Repeat to box the other corner.

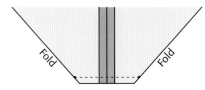

4. Add an inside pocket to one or both bag linings if desired. (See "Inside Pockets" on page 12.) Join the bag linings as in step 2, leaving 4" open in the bottom seam for turning. Sew the lining corners as in step 3.

5. Add a plastic canvas insert to the bottom of the bag. (See "Bottom Inserts" on page 13.)

6. Insert the lining into the bag, right sides together. Match the side seams and raw edges, and pin. Sew across the entire top of the bag, pivoting at the corners and sewing into the V

on each side. Clip into the seam allowance at each dot. Clip the corners. Turn right side out and press.

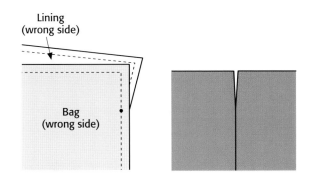

7. Close the opening and tack the lining to the bag. (See "Final Tacking" on page 15.) Fold down the top edge even with the dots so that the lining forms a 1"-wide contrasting band around the top of the bag. Topstitch the lower edge of the band to form a self-casing for the tubular frame.

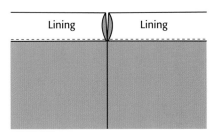

8. Use the fabric strap pieces and the fusible-fleece pieces to make two straps. (See "Making Shoulder Straps" on page 9.) Stitch upholstery trim down the middle of each strap and trim off the excess. Pin the raw edges of a strap to the bag front, slightly below the topstitched edge, as indicated on the pattern. Stitch in place over the topstitching. Repeat on the bag back.

9. Starting at a side seam, pin upholstery trim around the top of bag, concealing the topstitching and the strap ends. Cut off the excess and fold in the end. Topstitch.

10. Insert the tubular frame into the casing. (See "Inserting a Tubular Frame" on page 9.)

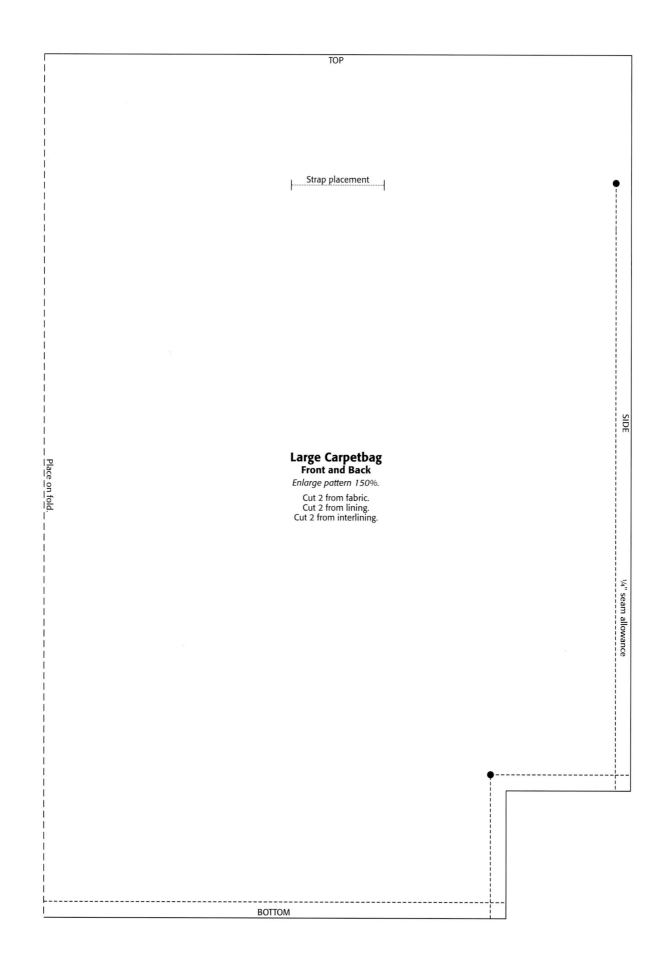

TOP

Strap placement

SIDE

¼" seam allowance

Place on fold.

Large Carpetbag
Front and Back
Enlarge pattern 150%.

Cut 2 from fabric.
Cut 2 from lining.
Cut 2 from interlining.

BOTTOM

SMALL CARPETBAG

SMALL CARPETBAG

If you like the luggage look of a carpetbag but don't need a big bag, try this smaller version. At 12" x 9" x 4" deep, it's just the ticket for quick excursions.

MATERIALS

The yardage is based on a 42" width. In addition to the items below, you'll need the general supplies listed on page 13.

- ⅔ yard of black polka-dot fabric for bag
- ⅔ yard of green windowpane plaid for lining
- ¼ yard of green-and-black check for pocket and straps
- ⅛ yard of brown marbled print for trim
- ⅔ yard of interlining
- Fusible fleece for straps
- Heavyweight plastic needlepoint canvas
- Purchased 7" tubular frame

CUTTING

See "Cutting and Marking" on page 14. Transfer the pattern markings to the fabric pieces before you begin sewing.

From the bag fabric, cut:
2 pieces using the front and back pattern (page 73)

From the interlining, cut:
2 pieces using the front and back pattern

From the lining fabric, cut:
2 pieces using the front and back pattern

1 piece using the pocket pattern (page 73) for pocket lining

From the pocket/strap fabric, cut:
1 piece using the pocket pattern for pocket

2 pieces, 2½" x 15", for straps

From the trim fabric, cut:

1 piece, 2" x 6", for pocket trim

2 pieces, 1½" x 30", for strap/casing trim

From the fusible fleece, cut:

2 pieces, ¾" x 15", for straps

ASSEMBLY

1. Fuse or baste the interlining to the wrong side of each bag piece.

2. Layer the pocket piece and the pocket lining piece right sides together. Stitch around the curved edges using a ¼" seam allowance; leave the straight edge open. Turn and press. Hand baste the raw edges between the dots and gather slightly.

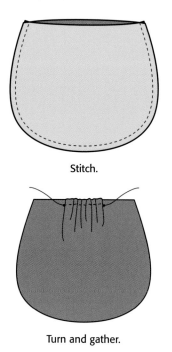

Stitch.

Turn and gather.

3. Press the long edges of the pocket trim ¼" to the wrong side. Fold the trim lengthwise in half, wrong sides together, matching the folded edges. Enclose the raw edge of the pocket inside the trim, letting the trim extend beyond the pocket at each end. Pin.

Topstitch the lower folded edge of the trim through all layers. Press the excess trim at each end toward the lining.

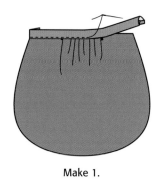

Make 1.

4. Pin the pocket to the bag front, right sides up. Topstitch the curved edge of the pocket. Add a second row of stitching ¼" from the edge.

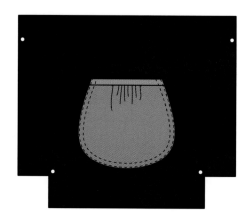

5. Follow "Assembly" steps 2–7 for the Large Carpetbag (page 69).

6. Use the fabric strap pieces and the fusible fleece pieces to make two straps. (See "Making Shoulder Straps" on page 9.)

7. Fold a strap/casing trim strip lengthwise in half, right sides together. Stitch the long edges using a ¼" seam allowance. Turn and press, centering the seam. Make two pieces.

8. Cut a trim piece from step 7 in half. Center one piece on a strap, seamed sides together. Topstitch both long edges. Make two straps with trim.

9. Pin the raw edges of a strap to the bag front, slightly below the topstitched edge, as indicated on the pattern. Stitch ¼" from the raw edge. Repeat on the bag back.

10. Starting at a side seam, pin the remaining trim piece from step 7 around the bag, concealing the topstitching and the strap ends. Cut off the excess and fold in the end. Topstitch both long edges.

11. Insert the tubular frame into the casing. (See "Inserting a Tubular Frame" on page 9.)

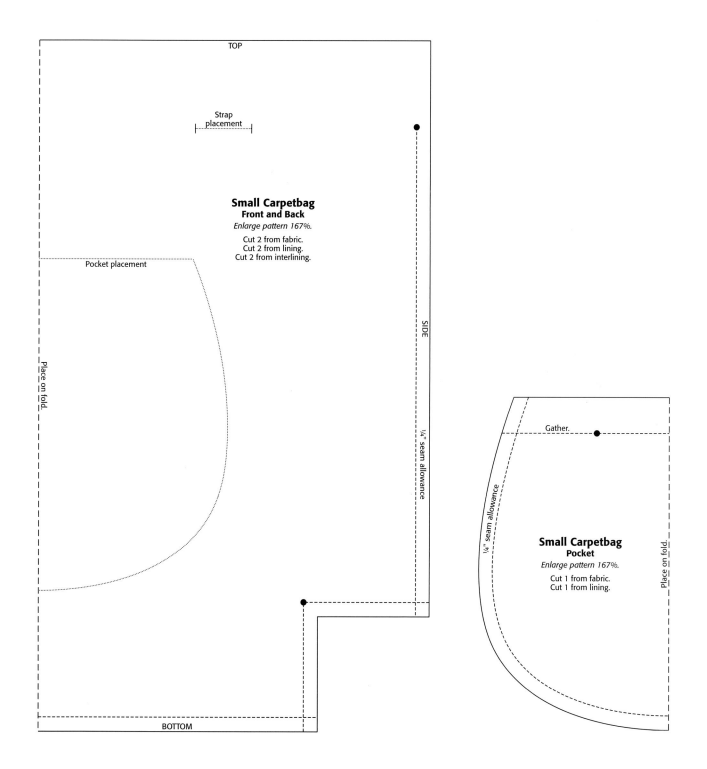

CHRISTY TOTE

CHRISTY TOTE

MATERIALS

The yardage is based on a 42" width. In addition to the items below, you'll need the general supplies listed on page 13.

- 1⅓ yards of denim for bag, lining, and patchwork, plus extra for pockets if desired
- 5 or 6 assorted ⅛-yard cuts, or scraps from your stash, of denim or chambray shirting for patchwork
- ¼ yard of floral print for flower
- ¾ yard of fusible interfacing, 22" wide
- Contrasting sewing thread
- Magnetic snap closure
- Heavyweight plastic needlepoint canvas
- Button for flower center

CUTTING

See "Cutting and Marking" on page 14. Cut each piece with the longer edge on the lengthwise fabric grain. Transfer the pattern markings to the fabric pieces before you begin sewing.

From the denim, cut:
1 piece, 15¼" x 21½", for bag lining
1 piece, 8½" x 15¼", for bag bottom
1 piece, 4" x 26", for strap
2 pieces, 3" x 16", for patchwork

A large tote with a patchwork body is perfect for your recycled fabrics. Choose denim and striped shirting fabrics, as shown, or assemble other hard-wearing fabrics from your stash or rummage sale finds. You need just a small amount of each fabric to piece the striped area of the design. The tote is 13" x 7" x 3" deep.

From the assorted fabrics, cut:
6 pieces, 3" x 16", for patchwork

From the fusible interfacing, cut:
1 piece, 16" x 16", for patchwork interlining
1 piece, 6" x 8", for flower

From the floral print, cut:
2 pieces, 6" x 8", for flower

ASSEMBLY

1. Lay out six assorted 3" x 16" pieces side by side in an arrangement you like. Place a 3" x 16" denim strip at each end. Sew the pieces together along the long edges using a ⅝" seam allowance. Press the seams open.

2. Thread the sewing machine with contrasting thread. Sew a zigzag stitch over each seam from the right side. Use a straight stitch to sew random curved lines across the surface of the patchwork. Add decorative machine stitches, if desired. Press well.

3. Fuse the interfacing to the wrong side of the patchwork. Trim off the excess interfacing, even with the edge of the patchwork.

4. Cut the patchwork in half to make two pieces, each 8" x 15¼", for the bag front and the bag back.

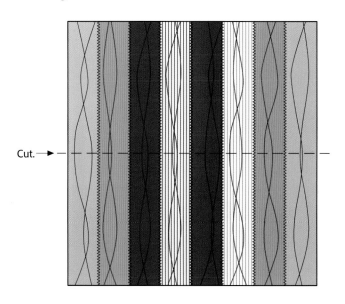

5. Layer the bag front and the bag bottom right sides together. Stitch one long edge using a ⅝" seam allowance. Press the seam open. Join the bag back to the bag bottom in the same way. Zigzag the seams with contrasting thread.

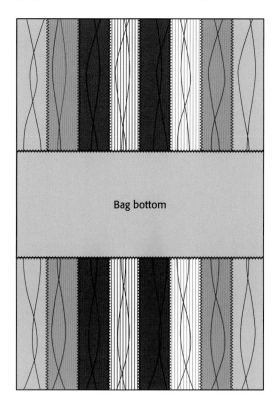

6. Measure the piece made in step 5. Trim the lining piece so that its width is ½" smaller. Making the lining slightly narrower than the bag will ensure a smooth, snug fit.

7. Fold the bag in half, right sides together. Sew the side edges using a ⅝" seam allowance. Press the seams open. Lightly press the fold line.

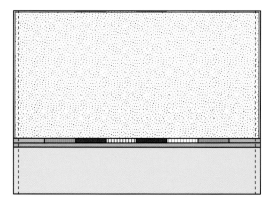

8. To form the bottom corners, refold the bag, right sides together, aligning the side seam on the pressed-in fold. Stitch straight across the corner, perpendicular to the seam line and about 1¾" from the point. Repeat to box the other corner.

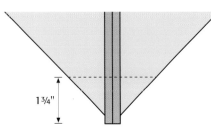

9. Add a pocket to the bag lining if desired. (See "Inside Pockets" on page 12.) Sew the bag lining as in step 7. Sew the lining corners as in step 8.

10. Add a plastic canvas insert to the bottom of the bag. (See "Bottom Inserts" on page 13.)

11. Press each long edge of the strap piece ½" to the wrong side. Fold the strap piece lengthwise in half, wrong sides together and folded edges matching. Topstitch the long edges with contrasting thread. Sew a wide zigzag stitch in contrasting thread down the middle of the strap.

12. Center the ends of the strap on the side seams of the lining, right sides together and raw edges aligned. Pin. Sew an X pattern to secure the straps to the lining.

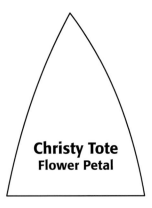

13. Turn the bag right side out. Turn the lining wrong side out. Insert the lining into the bag, wrong sides together. Fold in the top edge of the bag 1¼". Fold the top edge of the lining to match. Press to set the folds. Remove the lining from the bag and add a magnetic snap closure. (See "Inserting Magnetic Snaps" on page 8.) Reinsert the lining in the bag, tucking the corners toward the bottom. Zigzag around the top edges. Tack the lining to the bag at the corners. (See "Final Tacking" on page 15.)

14. Following the manufacturer's instructions for fusible web, fuse the floral print pieces back to back.

15. Trace seven flower petal patterns (below) onto the floral print piece, spacing them at least ½" apart. Stitch each petal outline with contrasting thread. Cut out each petal ⅛" beyond the stitching line.

16. Thread a needle with an 18" length of thread. Pinch the base of a petal toward its center and secure with a few stitches. Pinch the base of another petal. Pass the needle through the pinch, slide the petal close to the first petal, and secure with a few more tacking stitches. Continue adding petals in this way, shaping the flower as you go, until all the petals are joined. Tack firmly from the underside.

17. Sew the button to the flower center to conceal the tacking. Tack the flower to the bag front, centering it just below the top edge.

Christy Tote
Flower Petal

LOUISE BAG

LOUISE BAG

This petite bag offers a big opportunity for creative fabric recycling. The body of the bag is pieced from three different red print fabrics, but you could easily use more. A flirty polka-dot lining peeks out through a V-shaped opening at the top of each side seam. The size is just 5½" x 4" x 2" deep.

MATERIALS

The yardage is based on a 42" width. In addition to the items below, you'll need the general supplies listed on page 13.

- ⅓ yard of mediumweight to heavyweight striped fabric for bag, straps, and patchwork
- ⅜ yard of fabric for lining
- ⅛ yard each of 2 different prints, or scraps from your stash, for patchwork
- ½ yard of fusible interfacing, 22" wide
- Magnetic snap closure
- Heavyweight plastic needlepoint canvas
- Contrasting sewing thread
- Vintage button

CUTTING

See "Cutting and Marking" on page 14. Cut each fabric piece with the longer edge on the lengthwise grain. Transfer the pattern markings to the fabric pieces before you begin sewing.

From the striped fabric, cut:
2 pieces, 3" x 13", for patchwork
2 pieces, 3" x 22", for straps

From the prints, cut:
2 pieces, 2¾" x 13", from 1 print
1 piece, 2¾" x 13", from the other print

From the fusible interfacing, cut:

1 piece, 10" x 14", for patchwork interlining

2 pieces, 2½" x 22", for straps

From the lining fabric, cut:

1 piece using the bag pattern (page 80)

ASSEMBLY

1. Lay out the print pieces side by side with the matching pieces on the outside. Place a striped 3" x 13" piece at each end. Sew the pieces together along the long edges using a ⅝" seam allowance. Press the seams open.

2. Thread the sewing machine with contrasting thread. Zigzag each seam from the right side. Use a straight stitch to sew random curved lines across the surface of the patchwork. You can also use decorative machine stitches. Press well.

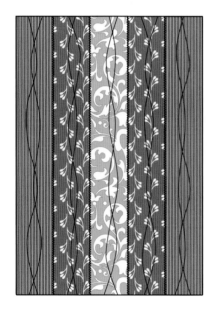

3. Fuse the 10" x 14" interfacing to the wrong side of the patchwork. Fold the patchwork

in half, align the bag pattern on the fold, and pin. Cut out one bag pattern piece.

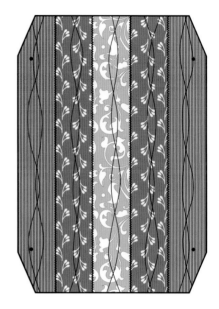

4. Measure the piece made in step 3. Trim the lining piece so that its width is ½" smaller. Making the lining slightly narrower than the bag will ensure a smooth, snug fit.

5. Fold the bag piece in half, right sides together. Sew the side edges from the dot to the fold line using a ⅝" seam allowance. Press the seams open. Lightly press the fold line at the bottom of the bag.

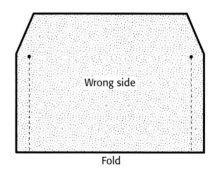

Wrong side

Fold

6. To form the bottom corners, refold the bag, right sides together, aligning the side seam on the pressed-in fold. Stitch straight across

the corner, perpendicular to the seam line and about 1¾" from the point. Repeat to box the other corner.

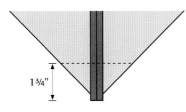

1¾"

7. Add a small pocket to the bag lining if desired. (See "Inside Pockets" on page 12.) Sew the bag lining as in step 5. Sew the lining corners as in step 6.

8. Add a plastic canvas insert to the bottom of the bag. (See "Bottom Inserts" on page 13.)

9. Turn the bag wrong side out. Turn the lining right side out. Insert the lining into the bag right sides together. Pin the angled edges together. Stitch from the dot to the top edge. Repeat to sew each angled edge. Clip into the seam allowance at the point of the V. Clip again on each side of the first clip. Turn the bag and lining right side out. Tuck the lining down into the bag. Press. Tuck in the top edges of the bag and lining ½" and press.

10. Install a magnetic snap in the lining about 1" from the top edge. (See "Inserting Magnetic Snaps" on page 8.)

11. Center a strap interfacing piece on the wrong side of a fabric strap piece. Fuse in place. Press each long edge of the strap piece ½" to the wrong side. Fold the strap piece in half lengthwise, wrong sides together and folded edges matching. Press. Topstitch the long edges. Sew a wide zigzag stitch down each edge in contrasting thread. Make two straps.

12. Unfold the top edge of the bag front. Pin the ends of a strap to the right side of the bag front, raw edges aligned. Zigzag the ends. Repeat for the bag back. Fold the top edges back in. Zigzag around the top edge to secure the bag to the lining. Sew a button to the bag front.

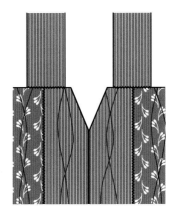

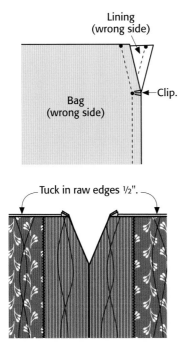

Lining
(wrong side)

Bag
(wrong side)

←Clip.

Tuck in raw edges ½".

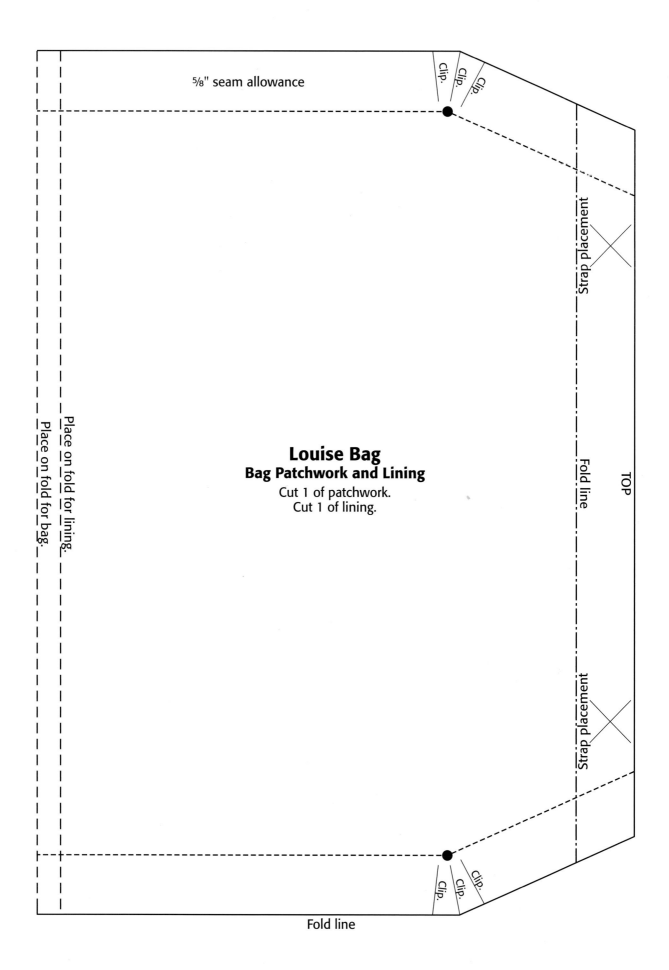

⅝" seam allowance

Clip.
Clip.
Clip.

Strap placement

Fold line

TOP

Louise Bag
Bag Patchwork and Lining
Cut 1 of patchwork.
Cut 1 of lining.

Place on fold for lining.
Place on fold for bag.

Strap placement

Clip.
Clip.
Clip.

Fold line

KATHLEEN BAG

COUNTRY KATHLEEN BAG
CITY KATHLEEN BAG

This bag is at home in the city or the country—just use fabrics and trim to dress it up or down. The patchwork squares let you showcase upholstery remnants from your fabric stash. Each bag is 13" x 15" x 4" deep.

MATERIALS

The yardage is based on a 42" width, unless noted. In addition to the items below, you'll need the general supplies listed on page 13.

- 12 assorted fabric scraps, at least 5½" x 5½"

- ½ yard or ¾ yard* of coordinating fabric for top band, bottom, and handles

- ⅝ yard of fabric for lining, plus extra for pockets if desired

- 1 yard of fusible interfacing, 22" wide

- 1 yard of fringe, 1" wide

- Heavyweight plastic needlepoint canvas

- Magnetic snap closure (optional)

*Choose the longer yardage to cut the pieces on the lengthwise grain.

CUTTING

See "Cutting and Marking" on page 14. There are no pattern pieces for this bag.

From the assorted scraps, cut:
12 squares, 5½" x 5½", for patchwork

From the coordinating fabric, cut:
2 pieces, 3" x 15½", for top band
2 pieces, 2½" x 15½", for bag bottom
2 pieces, 3" x 21", for handles

From the fusible interfacing, cut:

2 pieces, 15¼" x 15½", for bag front and back

2 pieces, 1" x 21", for handles

From the lining fabric, cut:

2 pieces, 15¼" x 15½", for bag front and back

ASSEMBLY

1. Arrange six assorted fabric squares in two rows of three squares each. Join the squares together in rows using a ¼" seam allowance. Press the seam allowances in the top row toward the middle. Press the seam allowances in the bottom row toward the outside edges. Sew the rows together. Press open. Repeat to make two patchwork pieces.

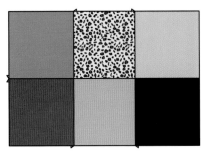

Make 2.

2. Layer a top band piece on the top edge of a patchwork unit, right sides together. Stitch using a ¼" seam allowance. Press toward the patchwork piece. Join a bottom piece to the lower edge of the patchwork in the same way. Make one bag front piece and one bag back piece.

3. Fuse an interfacing piece to the wrong side of the bag front. Cut out a 2" x 2" square from each lower corner. Repeat for the bag back.

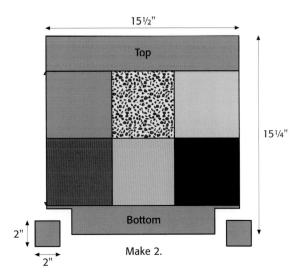

Make 2.

4. Layer the bag front and bag back pieces right sides together. Stitch one side seam using a ¼" seam allowance. Press open. Lay the bag flat, right side up. Pin the fringe across the bag, concealing the top band/pieced bag seam line. Stitch in place. Layer the bag right sides together again and sew the remaining side seam and the bottom seam. Do not stitch the cutout corners.

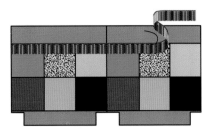

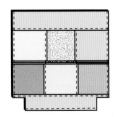

5. To form the bottom corners, refold the bag, right sides together, aligning a side seam on the bottom seam. Stitch the raw edges

together, using a ¼" seam allowance. Repeat to box the other corner. Turn right side out. Press.

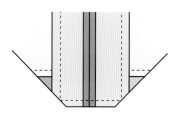

6. Cut out a 2" x 2" square from both lower corners of the bag front and back lining pieces as in step 3. Add a pocket to one or both of the lining pieces if desired. (See "Inside Pockets" on page 12.) Add a magnetic snap closure to the lining if desired, placing it 2½" from the top edge. (See "Inserting Magnetic Snaps" on page 8.) Join the lining pieces as in step 4, leaving 6" open in the bottom seam for turning. Box the lining corners as in step 5.

7. Add a plastic canvas insert to the bottom of the bag. (See "Bottom Inserts" on page 13.)

8. Center a fusible interfacing handle piece on the wrong side of a fabric handle piece. Fuse in place. Fold the handle piece in half lengthwise, right sides together. Stitch the long edges together using a ¼" seam allowance. Turn right side out. Press, centering the seam. Topstitch down the center of the handle and close to each long edge. Make two.

9. Pin the raw edges of a strap to the top edge of the bag front, 4" in from each side seam. Baste. Repeat for the bag back.

10. Turn the bag wrong side out. Turn the lining right side out. Insert the lining into the bag, matching the side seams and raw edges. Pin. Stitch the raw edges together all around using a ½" seam allowance. Turn right side out. Fold the lining over the seam allowance so that a ½"-wide band of lining fabric shows around the top edge of the bag. Stitch in the ditch all around. Press.

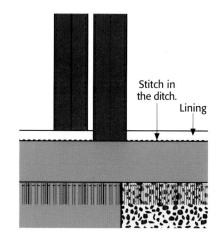

Stitch in the ditch.

Lining

11. Close the opening and tack the lining to the bag. (See "Final Tacking" on page 15.)

Leather Handles

To add leather handles as shown here, follow "Cutting" on page 81, with the following change: Omit the fabric and interfacing handles. Instead, use two purchased leather handles or cut two 21"-long pieces from two leather belts. Choose belts that show rich, warm color on both sides.

1. Follow "Assembly" steps 1–7 on page 82.

2. Machine baste a leather handle to the bag front, 4" in from each side seam, as in "Assembly" step 9. Repeat for the bag back.

3. Follow "Assembly" steps 10–11 to complete the bag.

MARGARET BAG

MARGARET BAG

Remember clutch bags from the 1960s with their cute cutout handles? Create the same look today using Timtex interfacing. It gives the bag and handles just the right amount of stiffness. Finish the raw edges of the handle cutout with machine satin stitches for a truly professional look. We always prepare scrap samples of the stiffened bag fabric for sewing practice. A practice piece lets us adjust the stitch width and length before we sew the actual bag. The bag is 8" x 10" x 3⅛" deep.

MATERIALS
The yardage is based on a 42" width, unless noted. In addition to the items below, you'll need the general supplies listed on page 13.

- ½ yard of fabric for lining and binding, plus extra for pockets if desired
- ⅜ yard of fabric for bag
- ¾ yard of Timtex interfacing, 22" wide
- Shortcut to Style heat-set crystals and rhinestuds
- Shortcut to Style Stone Styler heat-set tool
- Serger (optional)
- Spray fabric adhesive

CUTTING
See "Cutting and Marking" on page 14. Transfer the pattern markings to the fabric pieces before you begin sewing.

From the bag fabric, cut:
2 pieces using the front and back pattern (page 86)

From the Timtex interfacing, cut:
2 pieces using the front and back pattern

From the lining fabric, cut:
2 pieces using the front and back pattern

1 piece, 2½" x 30", for binding

ASSEMBLY

1. Spray one side of a Timtex piece with fabric adhesive, following the manufacturer's instructions. Layer the bag front piece right side up on the Timtex piece, carefully aligning the handle cutout and outside edges. Smooth in place. Press with a warm, dry iron.

2. Spray the Timtex side of the bag front with fabric adhesive. Place a lining piece on it, smooth in place, and press. Repeat steps 1 and 2 for the bag back.

3. Set the sewing machine for satin stitch. Using decorative thread, stitch around the handle cutout on the bag front, securing and enclosing the raw edges. Repeat for the bag back.

4. Layer the bag front and bag back right sides together. Satin stitch or serge the side and bottom edges. Do not stitch the cutout corners.

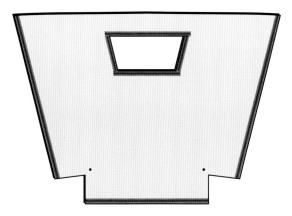

5. To form the bottom corners, refold the bag, right sides together, aligning a side seam on the bottom seam. Stitch the raw edges from dot to dot, using a ¼" seam allowance. Repeat to box the other corner. Turn right side out. Press.

6. Fold the binding piece in half lengthwise, wrong sides together. Starting ½" beyond a side seam, pin the binding strip to the purse, right sides together and raw edges aligned. Beginning at the side seam, stitch the binding to the top of the bag using a ¼" seam allowance. When you reach the starting point, cut off the excess, fold in the end, and slip-stitch the end for a neat finish.

7. Fold the binding onto the lining side of the bag to conceal the seam allowance. On the right side, topstitch ¼" below the seam line through all layers.

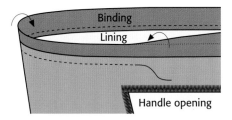

TIP: Read the manufacturer's instructions before pressing and washing items made with Timtex interfacing.

8. Embellish your fabric with decorative stones for a professional finish! Use tweezers to position a crystal on the fabric. Apply the heat-set tool to the crystal for about 20 seconds. Remove the tool and check to see if the crystal is stuck to the fabric. Reapply the tool to the crystal if necessary.

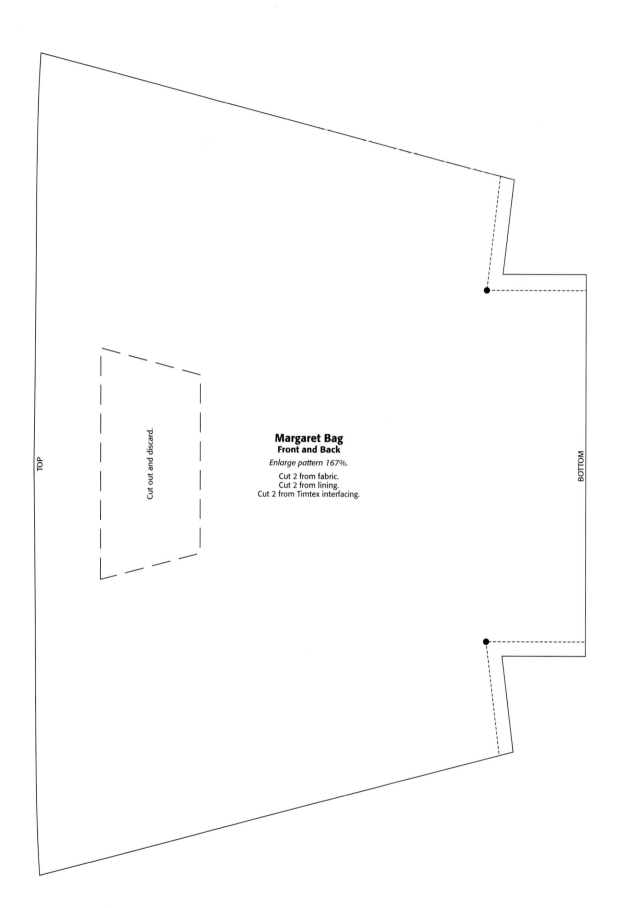

TOP

BOTTOM

Cut out and discard.

Margaret Bag
Front and Back

Enlarge pattern 167%.

Cut 2 from fabric.
Cut 2 from lining.
Cut 2 from Timtex interfacing.

MILDRED BAG

MILDRED BAG

MATERIALS

The yardage is based on a 42" width. In addition to the items below, you'll need the general supplies listed on page 13.

- 8 assorted fabrics, ⅛ yard each
- ½ yard of fabric for lining, plus extra for pockets if desired
- ¼ yard of fabric for top band
- ¼ yard of fabric for handles
- ½ yard of interlining
- Fusible fleece
- Magnetic snap closure (optional)
- 1 yard of piping or narrow trim
- Zipper foot

CUTTING

See "Cutting and Marking" on page 14. Transfer the pattern markings to the fabric pieces before you begin sewing.

From each of the assorted fabrics, cut:
1 piece, 2½" x 30" (8 pieces total)

From the interlining, cut:
1 piece, 16" x 30"
2 pieces using the top band pattern (page 89)

From the top band fabric, cut:
2 pieces using the top band pattern

From the lining fabric, cut:
2 pieces using the front and back pattern (page 90)

From the handle fabric, cut:
2 pieces, 3" x 20", for handles

From the fusible fleece, cut:
2 pieces, 1" x 20", for handles

Sew these dashing patchwork stripes using fabrics from your stash. A curved band creates a yoke effect across the top of the bag. Add a decorative trim, like the beaded fringe trim shown here, at the base of the yoke. The bag is a roomy 14" x 14".

ASSEMBLY

1. Lay out the eight assorted 2½" x 30" pieces side by side in an arrangement you like. Sew the pieces together along the long edges using a ¼" seam allowance. Press the seams open.

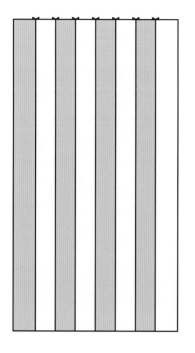

2. Fuse the interlining piece to the wrong side of the patchwork piece. They will not line up perfectly.

3. Fold the patchwork piece in half, right sides together, with the fold parallel to the seams. Align the front and back pattern on the fold and cut out one piece for the bag front. Repeat to cut the bag back.

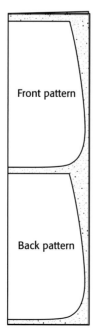

Front pattern

Back pattern

4. Fuse an interlining piece to the wrong side of each top band piece. Place the raw edge of the piping on the curved lower raw edge of a top band piece. Stitch using a zipper foot. Clip the curves. Press the seam allowance to the wrong side of the top band piece. Make two.

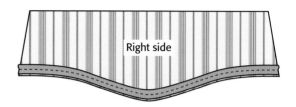

Right side

5. Place a top band piece on the bag front, right sides up. Baste the top and side edges. Stitch in the ditch along the curved edge of the band. Repeat for the bag back.

Stitch in the ditch.

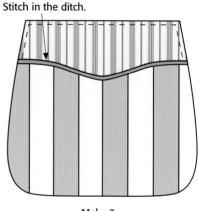

Make 2.

6. Layer the bag front and bag back right sides together. Stitch the curved edge all around using a ¼" seam allowance; leave the top edge open.

7. Add a pocket to one or both bag linings if desired. (See "Inside Pockets" on page 12.) Add a magnetic snap closure to the lining if desired. (See "Inserting Magnetic Snaps" on page 8.) Join the bag lining pieces as in step 6, leaving 5" open in the bottom seam for turning.

8. Use the handle pieces and the fusible-fleece strips to make two padded handles. Add three rows of stitching. (See "Making Shoulder Straps" on page 9.)

9. Center the raw edges of a handle strap on the top edge of the bag front at the mark. Baste. Repeat for the bag back.

10. Join the lining. (See "Joining the Lining" on page 15.) Fold the top outside edge of the bag ¼" to the inside. Topstitch ¼" from the top edge of the bag all around. Tack the lining to the bag. (See "Final Tacking" on page 15.)

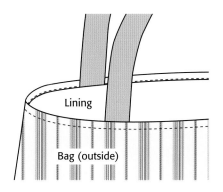

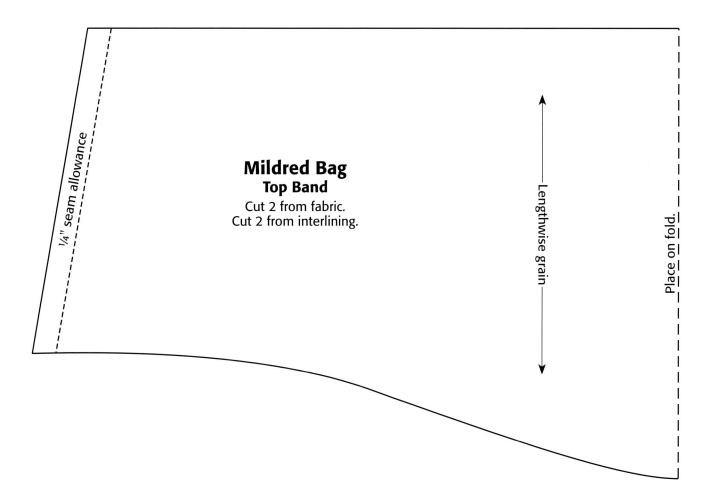

Mildred Bag
Top Band
Cut 2 from fabric.
Cut 2 from interlining.

¼" seam allowance

Lengthwise grain

Place on fold.

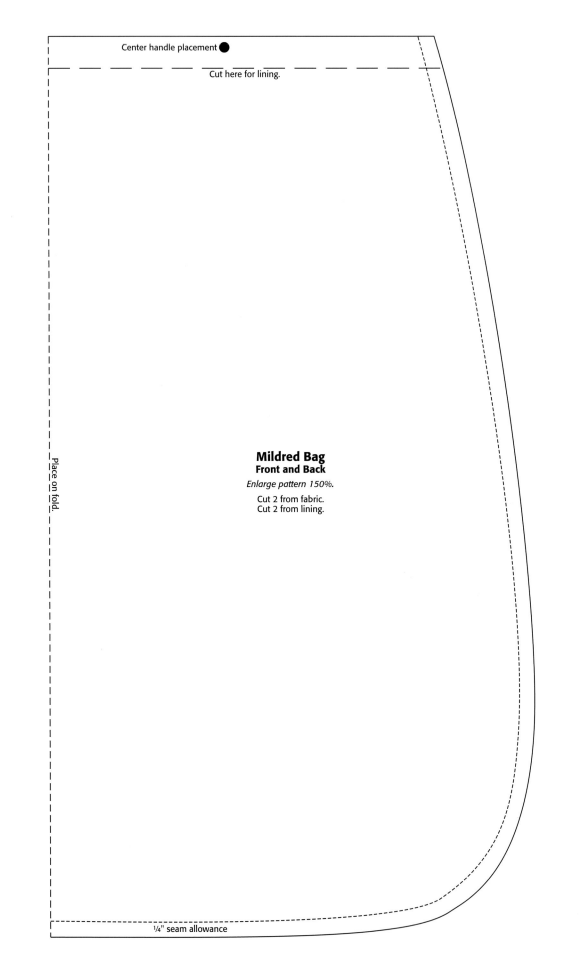

Center handle placement ●

Cut here for lining.

Place on fold

Mildred Bag
Front and Back

Enlarge pattern 150%.

Cut 2 from fabric.
Cut 2 from lining.

¼" seam allowance

SARA LOUISE BAG

BUTTON-FLAP SARA LOUISE BAG
MONOGRAM SARA LOUISE BAG

Use four fat quarters to make this patchwork bag. A variation project lets you add a machine-embroidered monogram. Finished size is 7" x 12" x 3" deep.

Use the instructions that follow to make the Button-Flap version of the bag. For directions on making the Monogram variation, see page 93.

MATERIALS

The yardage is based on a 42" width. In addition to the items below, you'll need the general supplies listed on page 13.

- 5 coordinating fat quarters of fabric for bag
- 2 matching fat quarters of fabric for lining
- ⅜ yard of interlining
- 1" button
- Heavyweight plastic needlepoint canvas

CUTTING

See "Cutting and Marking" on page 14. Transfer the pattern markings to the fabric pieces before you begin sewing.

From fat quarter 1, cut:
2 pieces using the lower front and back pattern (page 94)

From fat quarter 2, cut:
2 pieces, 3½" x 12", for top band

From fat quarter 3, cut:
2 pieces, 3" x 19", for handles

From fat quarter 4, cut:
2 pieces, 3¾" x 7", for center band

From fat quarter 5, cut:
2 pieces using the flap pattern (page 95)

From the interlining, cut:
1 piece using the flap pattern

Additional pieces will be cut in step 3.

ASSEMBLY

1. Press the long edges of a center band piece ¼" to the wrong side. Place the center band on the bag lower-front piece, right sides up. Topstitch the center band along both long edges. Repeat for the bag back.

2. Join a top band piece to the bag lower front using a ¼" seam allowance. Press toward the lower bag. Repeat for the bag back.

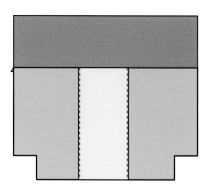

Make 2.

3. Use the pieced bag front from step 2 as a template to cut two front and back bag pieces from fat quarter 4 for the lining and two front and back bag pieces from the interlining.

4. Fuse or baste a bag interlining piece to the wrong side of the pieced bag front and the pieced bag back.

5. Layer the interlined bag front and bag back pieces right sides together. Stitch the side and bottom edges using a ¼" seam allowance. Do not stitch the cutout corners. Press the seams open.

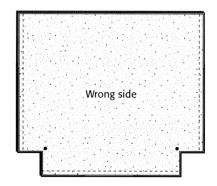

6. To form the bottom corners, refold the bag, right sides together, aligning a side seam on the bottom seam. Stitch the raw edges from dot to dot, using a ¼" seam allowance. Repeat to box the other corner. Turn right side out. Press.

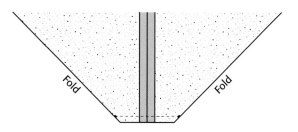

7. Add a pocket to one or both of the lining pieces if desired. (See "Inside Pockets" on page 12.) Join the lining pieces as in step 5, leaving 5" open in the bottom seam for turning. Sew the lining corners as in step 6.

8. Fuse or baste the interlining flap piece to the wrong side of a fabric flap piece. Layer the plain and interlined flap pieces right sides together. Stitch the side and bottom edges using a ¼" seam allowance; leave the top edge open. Clip the corners. Turn and press. Sew a buttonhole in the flap.

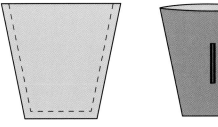

Make 1.

9. Fold a handle piece in half lengthwise, wrong sides together, and press. Open the handle piece. Fold in the long raw edges to meet at the center fold. Press. Refold the strap, right side out, with the long side edges tucked in. Topstitch the long edges through all layers. Make two.

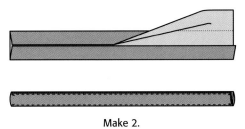
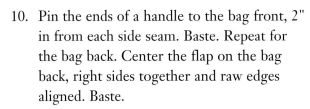

Make 2.

10. Pin the ends of a handle to the bag front, 2" in from each side seam. Baste. Repeat for the bag back. Center the flap on the bag back, right sides together and raw edges aligned. Baste.

11. Add a plastic canvas insert to the bottom of the bag. (See "Bottom Inserts" on page 13.) Join and tack the lining. (See "Joining the Lining" on page 15 and "Final Tacking" on page 15.) Topstitch ¼" from the top edge of the bag all around.

12. Sew the button to the bag front to match the buttonhole in the flap.

Monogram Sara Louise Bag

For a machine-embroidered monogram, we used a letter from "Antique Alphabet Letters" by The Vintage Workshop from Oklahoma Embroidery Supply and Design. In addition to machine embroidery thread, you'll need ¾ yard of jumbo rickrack and a magnetic snap. Follow "Cutting" on page 92, with the following changes:

- Cut the lower bag pieces from a gold stripe.
- Cut the center band pieces from a white and yellow stripe.
- Cut the top band from a gold plaid.
- Cut the handles from a coordinating gold plaid.
- Set aside a solid gold (2 fat quarters of the same fabric) for the lining .
- Omit the flap fabric and flap interlining pieces.

1. Follow "Assembly" step 1 on page 92 to sew the center band. Embroider the monogram on the center band through both layers of fabric.

2. Follow "Assembly" steps 2–4 .

3. Layer the interlined bag front and bag back pieces right sides together. Stitch one side seam using a ¼" seam allowance. Press open. Lay the bag flat, right side up. Pin the jumbo rickrack across the bag, concealing the top band/bag seam line. Stitch in place. Layer the bag right sides together again and sew the remaining side seam and bottom seam as in "Assembly" step 5.

4. Follow "Assembly" steps 6 and 7. In step 7, add a magnetic snap closure to the lining. (See "Inserting Magnetic Snaps" on page 8.)

5. Follow "Assembly" steps 9–11 to complete the bag.

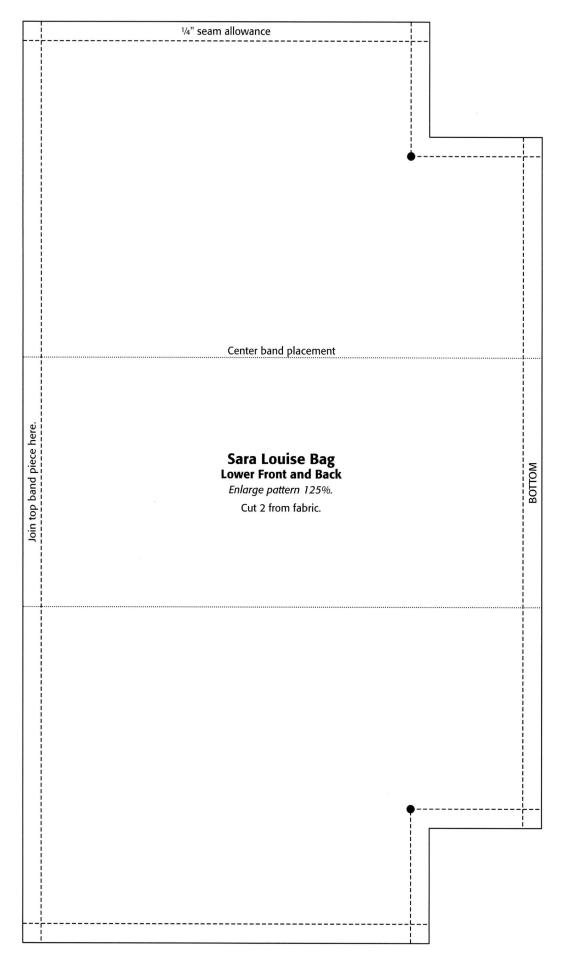

¼" seam allowance

Center band placement

Join top band piece here.

Sara Louise Bag
Lower Front and Back
Enlarge pattern 125%.
Cut 2 from fabric.

BOTTOM

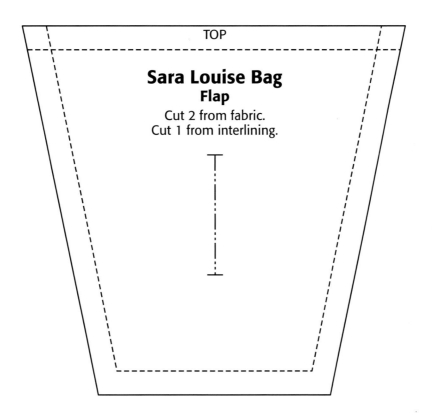

TOP

Sara Louise Bag
Flap
Cut 2 from fabric.
Cut 1 from interlining.

RESOURCES

Shop your local quilt and fabric stores for products from the following manufacturers who have graciously donated their products and materials for use in this book.

The Vintage Workshop is a division of Indygo Junction, Inc., that offers fashion images for embellishing handbags and wearables. For more information on The Vintage Workshop and to view our wonderful collection of images on CD-ROM, please visit our Web site at www.thevintageworkshop.com. Be sure to sign up to receive our free newsletter!

Indygo Junction is a publishing company that acts as an agency for more than 25 designers and artists whose work is recognized in the crafts industry. To date, Amy Barickman's company has published more than 400 patterns and 40 books that feature the work of many talented designers. This bag collection was designed by several of Amy's fabric artists.

Click-n-Craft CD-ROMs, Inkjet Printable Fabrics, Iron-on Transfers, Stone Styler Heat-Set Tool, and Heat-Set Crystals

The Vintage Workshop:
www.thevintageworkshop.com,
1-913-648-2700

Embroidery Designs

Oklahoma Embroidery Supply and Design:
www.embroideryonline.com

Fabrics

Dan River Fabrics: www.danriver.com
Moda Fabrics: www.unitednotions.com,
1-800-527-9447

Metal Purse Frames
(hex-open frame, tubular frame)

Ghee's: www.ghees.com, 1-318-226-1701

Patterns and Books

For a complete selection of great purse and wearable patterns as well as patterns for quilts and needlework, visit Indygo Junction, Inc.: www.indygojunctioninc.com, 1-913-341-5559

Purchased Handles and Notions
(magnetic snaps, feet, zippers, etc.)

Lacis: www.lacis.com, 1-510-843-7178
Darice: www.darice.com, 1-866-432-7423
Prym Dritz Bag Boutique: www.dritz.com
Clover Needlecraft, Inc.: www.clover-usa.com,
1-800-233-1703
Bagworks: www.bagworks.com, 1-800-365-7423

Ribbons and Trims

Trimtex Company, Inc.: www.saintlouistrim.com,
1-570-326-9135

Steam-A-Seam

The Warm Company: www.warmcompany.com,
1-206-320-9276

Timtex Interfacing

Timber Lane Press: www.timtexstore.com,
1-800-752-3353